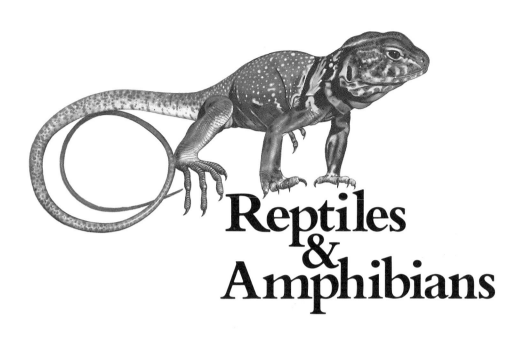

Reptiles
&
Amphibians

Longman Wildlife Library

Reptiles & Amphibians

Longman

Author: **Dr Philip Whitfield**, Zoology
Department, King's College, London

Consultant: **Professor Barry Cox**, Zoology
Department, King's College, London

Artist: **Alan Male**

Editor: **Jinny Johnson**
Text Editor: **Gwen Rigby**
Art Director: **John Bigg**
Researcher: **Pip Morgan**
Production: **Barry Baker**
           Janice Storr

Reptiles and Amphibians was conceived, edited
and designed by Marshall Editions Limited,
71 Eccleston Square, London SW1V 1PJ

Published by
Longman Group Limited,
Longman House, Burnt Mill, Harlow,
Essex CM20 2JE, England
and Associated Companies throughout the world

First published 1983
ISBN 0 582 55699 6

Filmset in *10/10*pt Goudy Old Style
by Filmtype Services Limited,
Scarborough, North Yorkshire

Printed in The Netherlands
by Koninklijke Smeets Offset B.V.

British Library Cataloguing in Publication Data
Reptiles and amphibians —— (Longman wildlife
  library)
  1. Reptiles 2. Amphibians
  I. Whitfield, P.
  597.9   QL665

ISBN 0 582 55699 6

CONSERVATION STATUS

Many of the world's animal species are in
danger of extinction or are becoming rare,
often as a direct result of human activity. By
destroying natural habitats, killing animals
for their fur or other uses, and by introduc-
ing predators into areas where they disturb
the natural ecological balance, we are in danger of losing for ever hundreds of species of
animals. All animals, particularly threatened
species, are monitored by the International
Union for Conservation of Nature and
Natural Resouces (IUCN) and listed in the
Red Data books that are produced by this
organization.

    The status of threatened species is in-
dicated in this book by symbols, the meaning of which is given in the next column.
This information is printed with the kind
assistance of the IUCN Conservation
Monitoring Centre, Cambridge, England.

SIZES: sizes given are the total length of the
animal unless otherwise stated. For turtles
and tortoises the length of the shell is given.

ENDANGERED Ⓔ

Species in grave danger of extinction and
which can only survive if effective conservation measures are adopted and the causes of
their difficulties cease.

VULNERABLE Ⓥ

Species which may become endangered if
the reduction in their numbers continues at
the present level.

RARE Ⓡ

Species which are at risk because their population is already small; for example, those
with restricted distribution.

OUT OF DANGER Ⓞ

Species which were once included in one of
the above categories but, because of effective
conservation measures, are now no longer in
danger.

INDETERMINATE Ⓘ

Species which are suspected of being endangered, vulnerable or rare, but about which
insufficient information is available.

Contents

Reptiles – survivors from a prehistoric age

The reptiles that still walk, burrow, climb and swim on our planet represent the survivors in a dramatic evolutionary history of reptilian experimentation. From amphibian beginnings some 300 million years ago, a wide range of more thoroughly terrestrial forms of vertebrate developed. These reptile starting-points have had far-reaching implications for the rest of vertebrate evolution. From these early reptile stocks our modern reptiles came. From them, too, however, came a plethora of magnificent dead-ends, including the once-mighty dinosaurs, the winged pterosaurs and the swimming ichthyosaurs and plesiosaurs. And from the midst of the complex early family tree of reptile prototypes developed the ancestors of the remaining two groups of terrestrial higher vertebrates: the mammals and the birds. Reptiles thus link the beginnings of life on land, the amphibians, with the most advanced and sophisticated vertebrates.

Different systems exist for classifying the class Reptilia. Most, however, recognize about 16 or 17 orders, known by fossils alone or from fossils and still existing animals. Only four orders persist today: first, the chelonians — turtles and tortoises; second, the crocodilians; third, the Squamata, which includes all lizards, snakes and the amphisbaenids; fourth, with only one living representative, the Rhynchocephalia or tuatara order. Even though these four orders represent only a small fraction of past reptilian diversity, they still show something of the interesting variation of which the reptile body form is capable.

The chelonians are a varied and successful assemblage of reptiles with about 230 known species. They have short, broad bodies, enclosed by a bony box into which, to a variable extent, head, tail and limbs can be retracted for protection. The protective box consists of internal bony plates upon which is superimposed tough, horny material, similar to the scales of other reptiles. Chelonians have no teeth but consume vegetation or prey items by grasping the foods with the sharp edges of a beak, developed from the upper and lower jaws.

Crocodiles and their allies are the only remaining representatives of the archosaurian reptiles. The archosaurs, in the form of dinosaurs and pterosaurs, were the dominant terrestrial animals on Earth from about 200 million years ago to approximately 63 to 70 million years ago. The characteristic elongate, heavy-headed crocodilians have been effective amphibious predators on earth for around 200 million years and are the largest living reptiles today. They are all carnivores, equipped with rows of sharp, peg-like teeth which are continually replaced as they become worn.

Lizards, snakes and the burrowing amphisbaenids make up the order Squamata, meaning the scaly ones. The elongate, slim, long-tailed bodies of lizards have become modified to enable them to live in a wide range of habitats. Lizards can be expert burrowers, runners, swimmers and climbers, and a few can manage crude, short-distance gliding on rib-supported "wings". Most are carnivores, feeding on invertebrate and small vertebrate prey, but others feed on vegetation. The elongate, limbless snakes have some of the most highly modified skulls to be found among vertebrates, with a high degree of flexibility to accommodate large prey and sometimes effective fang and venom systems. Other snakes use their long, powerful bodies to constrict and suffocate their prey in their embrace.

The final order of reptiles includes only the tuatara of New Zealand. It seems to have changed little in its essential details in 200 million years.

Each of the four orders of living reptiles shows different adaptations which mark a distinct advance from the amphibians. Perhaps the most crucial of these modifications relate to temperature control, skin structure and methods of reproduction.

Like the amphibians, reptiles seem not to have any significant ability to control their body temperature independently of external heat sources. They do, however, have a set of behaviour patterns which enables them to regulate the effect of external heat sources (sun, hot rocks) on their own temperature. By the use of specific postures and activities in or on the heat sources, reptiles can attain high body temperatures and regulate them to some degree. But their ultimate reliance on the sun for body heat means that the main bulk of reptile species occurs in tropical and warm temperate climates.

The moist skin of the amphibians is important as a respiratory surface. Reptiles, in contrast, have waterproofed themselves with a scaly outer layer that is physically and chemically tough and relatively impermeable to water.

Compared with amphibian methods of reproduction, those of all reptiles show a great leap forward in solving the problem of sexual reproduction on land. Instead of having to return to water to breed and being dependent on the water to bring eggs and sperm together, male reptiles fertilize their mates internally by means of their one or two penises.

The great reproductive advance of the reptiles, however, is their eggs with their tough shells, sometimes doubly strengthened with mineral salts to protect them from abrasion, damage and water loss in the soil where they are normally laid. The egg contains enough yolky food reserves and enough liquid to allow the reptile to develop directly into a miniature adult, instead of passing through an intermediate larval phase as do the amphibians. Systems of blood vessels, running in special membranes enclosing the embryo, transfer the food reserves to it, exchange oxygen and carbon dioxide with the outside air via the shell, or transfer nitrogenous waste products, to be deposited in a special sac that is left behind in the shell when the reptile hatches out. The hatchling has an egg tooth which it uses to slit open the shell and which it sheds afterwards.

In some reptiles, eggs are retained within the female's body and hatch within it or as they are laid, so that the female produces fully formed live young. In these species the shell is only a thin transparent membrane. A few reptiles and snakes have advanced still further, and their young develop inside the body with no shell membrane, having instead a primitive form of placenta. Young which develop inside the mother have many advantages in that they are protected from predators and physical dangers. By sunning herself, the mother can keep her body temperature as high as possible, in turn ensuring that the embryos develop rapidly. Live-bearing species occur even in predominantly egg-laying families and are often reptiles that live in particularly harsh climates or at high altitudes.

Reptiles in their evolution have produced all the basic adaptations necessary for efficient terrestrial life that the more advanced birds and mammals carry to higher levels of sophistication. Successful in their own right, they have provided the springboard for the even greater adaptive modifications of the body plans and abilities of the vertebrate animal.

Emydid Turtles

NAME: Pond Slider, *Pseudemys scripta*
RANGE: USA: Virginia to N. Florida, west to New Mexico; Central America to Brazil
HABITAT: slow rivers, ponds, swamps
SIZE: 13–30 cm (5–11¾ in)

Pond sliders are highly aquatic creatures, rarely moving far from water. They bask on floating logs, often lying on top of one another. The carapace is oval and the markings variable. Males are usually smaller than females and have elongated curved claws. Young pond sliders feed on insects, crustaceans, molluscs and tadpoles, but as they mature they feed more on plants.

In June and July pond sliders lay up to three clutches of 4 to 23 eggs each. Millions of these turtles are raised on farms and sold as pets.

NAME: False Map Turtle, *Graptemys pseudogeographica*
RANGE: USA: Minnesota to Sabine River area of Louisiana and Texas
HABITAT: rivers, lakes, ponds
SIZE: 8–25 cm (3–9¾ in)

False map turtles have intricate shell patterns and clear markings on their small heads. Males are smaller than females and have enlarged foreclaws. These turtles prefer habitats with plenty of vegetation and feed on aquatic plants as well as on crustaceans and molluscs.

After a courtship ritual, during which the male swims above the female then faces her and drums her snout with his claws, the pair mate. The nesting period is from May to July. The female turtle digs a pit in the soil of the river or lake bank with her hind feet and deposits her 6 to 15 eggs. Up to three clutches are laid in a season. The numbers of this once common species have been reduced by pollution of its habitats.

NAME: Diamondback Terrapin, *Malaclemys terrapin*
RANGE: USA: Atlantic and Gulf coasts
HABITAT: salt marshes, estuaries, lagoons
SIZE: 10–23 cm (4–9 in)

This terrapin is the only North American emydid adapted for life in brackish and salt water. It is a strong, fast-swimming turtle with large hind limbs. Females are bigger than males.

Diamondbacks spend their days on mud-flats or tidal marshes, feeding on snails, clams and worms and on some plant shoots. At night they bury themselves in mud, and in the northern part of their range they hibernate throughout the winter, buried in mud. Diamondbacks mate in the spring and lay 5 to 18 eggs in cavities which they dig in the marshes or dunes.

ORDER CHELONIA

This order contains all forms of turtles and tortoises, perhaps the most familiar of reptiles. There are about 230 living species. A typical chelonid has its body enclosed in a shell made of modified horny scales and bone. The shell is in two parts: the upper part on the animal's back is the carapace, and the shell underneath the body is the plastron. The ribs and most of the vertebrae are attached to the shell. Both pelvic and pectoral girdles lie within the shell and the limbs emerge sideways. The neck is long and flexible and can usually be withdrawn into the shell. In most families the neck bends up and down to retract, but in 2 families, the greaved turtles (Pelomedusidae), and the matamata and snake-necked turtles (Chelidae), the neck bends sideways when being retracted.

Chelonids have no teeth, but their jaws are equipped with horny beaks of varying strength. All lay eggs, usually burying them in a pit in sand or earth. Hatchlings must dig their own way out to the surface.

EMYDIDAE: Emydid Turtle Family

A varied group of freshwater and semi-terrestrial turtles, the emydid family is the largest group of living turtles, with around 85 species. The family is closely related to the land tortoises (Testudinidae); indeed, some authorities group them together as one family. A clear distinguishing feature of the emydid group is the adaptation of the hind feet for swimming rather than walking. Most species live in the northern hemisphere.

Emydid turtles have a varied diet and generally eat both plant and animal food. Some species start life as carnivores but feed mainly on plants as adults.

NAME: Wood Turtle, *Clemmys insculpta*
RANGE: USA: Nova Scotia to N. Virginia; Great Lakes region
HABITAT: woods, marshy meadows, swamps
SIZE: 12.5–23 cm (5–9 in)

The rough-shelled wood turtle spends most of its life on land but is usually in the vicinity of water. It is a good climber and feeds on fruit as well as on worms, slugs and insects. In May or June females lay 6 or 8 eggs, which usually hatch by October, but which may over-winter and hatch the following spring in the north. Adults hibernate in the north of the range. Wood turtles are popular pets, but they have been over-hunted and are now rare and protected in some states of the USA.

NAME: Eastern Box Turtle, *Terrapene carolina*
RANGE: USA: E. states, west to Texas
HABITAT: moist forested areas
SIZE: 10–20 cm (4–8 in)

A poor swimmer, the box turtle rarely enters any other than shallow water and spend most of its life on land. Its carapace is nearly always domed in shape and it is variable in coloration and pattern. Box turtles eat almost anything, but slugs, earthworms and fruit are favoured foods; they are able to eat mushrooms that are poisonous to humans, and anyone then eating the turtle is poisoned. Usually active early in the day or after rain, box turtles may take refuge in swampy areas in the heat of the summer.

In the spring, after hibernating throughout the winter, box turtles perform prolonged courtship rituals. The female lays 3 to 8 eggs in a flask-shaped pit which she digs. The hatchlings may remain in the nest over the following winter. Females can store sperm and lay fertile eggs several years after mating.

NAME: European Pond Turtle, *Emys orbicularis*
RANGE: central France, south to N. Africa, east to Iran
HABITAT: ponds, marshes, rivers
SIZE: 13–15 cm (5–6 in)

An aquatic species, the European pond turtle prefers water with plenty of vegetation, but suns itself on river banks and hunts prey on land as well as in water. It is entirely carnivorous and feeds on prey such as fish, frogs, snails and worms.

In winter these turtles hibernate, burying themselves in mud or in specially built chambers in the river bank. They mate in spring and, having dug an egg pit with her tail, the female lays 3 to 16 eggs. She generally uses the same nest site every year.

NAME: Batagur, *Batagur baska*
RANGE: S.E. Asia from Bengal to Vietnam
HABITAT: tidal areas, estuaries
SIZE: 58 cm (23 in) Ⓔ

A large herbivorous turtle with a smooth heavy shell, the batagur is often found in brackish or even salt water. It has only four claws on each foot.

Batagurs nest on sandbanks and usually lay three clutches in a season, making a total of 50 to 60 eggs. Excessive collecting of eggs and killing of adults for food has led to a decline in the population, and this turtle has now been eliminated in some parts of its range.

POND SLIDER

FALSE MAP TURTLE

BATAGUR

EASTERN BOX TURTLE

EUROPEAN POND TURTLE

DIAMONDBACK TERRAPIN

WOOD TURTLE

Land Tortoises

NAME: African Pancake Tortoise,
Malocochersus tornieri
RANGE: Africa: Kenya, Tanzania
HABITAT: rocky outcrops in arid land
SIZE: 15 cm (6 in) (I)

The African pancake tortoise is one of the world's most unusual and extraordinary species. Its shell is extremely flat and soft, and rather than retreating into its shell when disturbed, the tortoise runs to hide in a rock crevice. Once there, it inflates its lungs, thus increasing its size, so that it is wedged in and almost impossible to remove. It sometimes falls when clambering over rocks but can right itself easily because of its flat shell and slender, flexible limbs. Females are slightly larger than males.

The pancake tortoise feeds on dry grass. It nests in July and August, laying 1 egg at a time, and it may lay two or more times in a season. The eggs hatch after about 6 months.

NAME: Gopher Tortoise, *Gopherus*
polyphemus
RANGE: USA: S. Carolina to Florida,
west to Louisiana
HABITAT: sandy areas between grassland
and forest
SIZE: 23.5–37 cm (9¼–14½ in)

The gopher tortoise has a domed shell and heavily scaled front legs, flattened for efficient digging. An excellent burrower, this tortoise makes an unusually long tunnel, ending in a chamber which serves as a refuge where humidity and temperature remain relatively constant. One tunnel recorded was over 14 m (46 ft) long. Other small animals may move in and share the tortoise's burrow.

Gopher tortoises emerge from their burrows during the day to bask in the sun and feed on grass and leaves. They mate in spring and nest from April to July. Several clutches of 2 to 7 eggs are laid in a shallow pit during the nesting period.

NAME: Bowsprit Tortoise, *Chersine*
angulata
RANGE: South Africa
HABITAT: coastal areas
SIZE: 15–18 cm (6–7 in)

The bowsprit tortoise has distinctive triangular markings on its carapace. The front opening of the carapace is particularly small, providing good protection against predators. Males are bigger than females and aggressive toward one another. Bowsprits are believed to feed on plant material. They nest in August and lay 1 or 2 eggs in a hole about 10 cm (4 in) deep. The eggs usually take about a year to hatch.

TESTUDINIDAE:
Land Tortoise Family

There are about 39 species of land tortoise, found in North America, Europe and Asia, and in Africa and Madagascar. All are strictly terrestrial and have stumpy, elephantine hind legs; on the front legs are thick, hard scales. These tortoises can retract head and limbs completely inside the shell, leaving only the soles of the hind feet, tail region and scaly fronts of the forelimbs exposed. Thus most depend on their armour for protection and do not usually show aggression or attempt to flee when disturbed. All species are predominantly herbivorous.

NAME: Galápagos Giant Tortoise,
Geochelone elephantopus
RANGE: Galápagos Islands
HABITAT: varied, cool, moist forest to
arid land
SIZE: up to 1.2 m (4 ft) (E)

There are at least 13 subspecies of these giant tortoises, which may weigh over 225 kg (500 lb). Subspecies have evolved because the populations are isolated from one another on separate islands and, over thousands of years, have adapted to suit the particular conditions. The discovery of these subspecies on the different islands was one of the major observations that stimulated Darwin to start his speculations on the origin of species.

The tortoises vary in size, length and thickness of limbs and, most importantly, in the shape of the carapace. Some species have a "saddleback" shell which rises up above the head, allowing the tortoise to lift its head right up and so graze on a greater range of vegetation. These species occur only on those islands with high-growing vegetation. Males are always markedly larger than females.

Galápagos tortoises feed on almost any vegetation, which they seek in the more fertile highlands. They mate at any time of year, and males are easily able to overcome the smaller females and bear them to the ground for mounting. Nesting has been closely observed on Indefatigable Island where there is a tortoise reserve. After mating, the female descends to the lowland area, where there is bare soil in full sun; she then urinates to soften the earth and digs a pit up to 30.5 cm (12 in) deep with her hind feet. After laying up to 17 eggs, she plasters the excavated soil over the cavity so that it is well closed; the soil dries again in the sun. As usual with tortoises, the young must hatch and dig themselves out of the cavity unaided.

NAME: Leopard Tortoise, *Geochelone*
pardalis
RANGE: Africa: Sudan and Ethiopia to
South Africa
HABITAT: savanna, woodland
SIZE: 61 cm (24 in)

The leopard tortoise has a markedly domed, boldly patterned carapace. It feeds on a great variety of plant material, including fruit and beans. Courting males compete for females, butting at each other until one is overturned. They nest in September and October in South Africa, but the season is longer in tropical Africa. The female prepares a nest cavity by urinating on the soil to soften it, then excavating a pit with her hind limbs. She lays 5 to 30 eggs, and there may be several clutches in a season.

NAME: Schweigger's Hingeback Tortoise,
Kinixys erosa
RANGE: W. and central Africa
HABITAT: rain forest, marshes, river
banks
SIZE: 33 cm (13 in)

A unique hinge on the carapace of this tortoise, located in line with the junction of the second and third back plates, allows the rear of the carapace to be lowered, if the tortoise is attacked, to afford some protection to its hindquarters. This hinge is not present in young tortoises. By digging itself into plant debris, the hingeback remains hidden for much of its life. It feeds on plants and may also eat small animals. There are usually 4 eggs in a clutch.

NAME: Spur-thighed Tortoise, *Testudo*
graeca
RANGE: N. Africa; extreme S.E. and
S.W. Europe; Middle East
HABITAT: meadows, cultivated land,
woodland
SIZE: 15 cm (6 in) (V)

This tortoise has a moderately domed shell and a small spur in the thigh region of each front limb. Females are larger than males. The tortoises hibernate in winter but, in coastal areas, will emerge as early as February. They court in spring, the male butting and biting the female before mating with her. The eggs, usually 2 or 3 in a clutch, are laid in May and June and generally hatch in September and October, although this varies with the local climate. The young tortoises are similar to adults but have more rounded shells and clearer markings.

Thousands of these tortoises are collected and exported as pets, many of which die because of unsuitable climate and conditions.

SCHWEIGGER'S HINGEBACK TORTOISE

AFRICAN PANCAKE TORTOISE

GOPHER TORTOISE

GALAPAGOS GIANT TORTOISE

BOWSPRIT TORTOISE

SPUR-THIGHED TORTOISE

LEOPARD TORTOISE

Snapping Turtles, Mud Turtles, River Turtles

CHELYDRIDAE: Snapping Turtle Family

The 2 species in this family are both large predatory freshwater turtles. They have massive non-retractile heads and strong jaws.

NAME: Snapping Turtle, *Chelydra serpentina*
RANGE: S. Canada to Ecuador
HABITAT: marshes, ponds, rivers, lakes
SIZE: 20–47 cm (8–18½ in)

A highly aggressive species, the snapping turtle shoots its head forward with surprising speed while snapping its strong jaws. It feeds on all kinds of aquatic and bankside life, including fish, amphibians, mammals and birds, as well as on aquatic plants. Usually found in water with plenty of aquatic vegetation, the snapping turtle lies at the bottom, concealed among plants. It is an excellent swimmer. Males and females are alike in appearance, but males grow slightly larger.

Snapping turtles hibernate in winter and begin nesting in early summer. The average clutch is 25 to 50 eggs, laid in a flask-shaped cavity, dug by the female. As the eggs are laid, she pushes each one into place with movements of her hind feet. The eggs incubate for 9 to 18 weeks, depending on the area and the weather; in cooler areas, the hatchlings may remain in the nest through the winter.

NAME: Alligator Snapping Turtle, *Macroclemys temmincki*
RANGE: central USA
HABITAT: deep rivers, lakes
SIZE: 33–66 cm (13–26 in)

The alligator snapping turtle has three strong ridges on the carapace and a rough-textured head and neck. The carapace is shaped, allowing the head to be raised. A resident of dark, slow-moving water, this turtle is so sedentary that algae grow on its shell, contributing to the existing camouflage of the lumpy irregular outline. It rests, practically invisible to passing fishes, with its huge mouth gaping open to reveal a pink, fleshy appendage. Unsuspecting fish come to investigate the "bait" and are swallowed whole or sliced in half by the turtle's strong jaws. It also eats crustaceans.

These turtles continue to grow after maturity and some old specimens, at over 76 cm (30 in) long and 91 kg (200 lb) in weight, are the largest freshwater turtles in the USA. They nest between April and June and lay from 15 to 50 eggs in a flask-shaped pit dug near water. The young are born with a rough-surfaced shell and the lure already in place.

KINOSTERNIDAE: Mud and Musk Turtle Family

The 18 species in this family are mainly aquatic turtles living in North and Central America and northern South America. They give off a musky odour from 2 pairs of glands, positioned on each side of the body where skin and shell meet. Their heads are retractile.

NAME: Yellow Mud Turtle, *Kinosternon flavescens*
RANGE: USA: Nebraska to Texas; Mexico
HABITAT: slow streams
SIZE: 9–16 cm (3½–6¼ in)

The yellow mud turtle does indeed seem to prefer water with a mud bottom, but it may also be found in artificial habitats such as cattle drinking troughs and ditches. It feeds on both aquatic and terrestrial invertebrates. Breeding females lay 2 to 4 eggs.

NAME: Common Musk Turtle, *Sternotherus odoratus*
RANGE: USA: E. states, west to Texas
HABITAT: slow, shallow, muddy streams
SIZE: 8–13 cm (3–5 in)

Also known as the stinkpot, this turtle exudes a strong-smelling fluid from its musk glands when molested. It is a highly aquatic species, rarely found far from water, but it does emerge to bask on branches overhanging water. It feeds on carrion, insects and molluscs as well as on small amounts of fish and plants. Nesting is from February to June, depending on the latitude; females lay 1 to 9 eggs under trees, logs or dead leaves.

CARETTOCHELYIDAE: Plateless River Turtle Family

This was once a widespread family, as proved by fossils found in Europe, Asia and North America. There is now only 1 species with a restricted distribution.

NAME: New Guinea Plateless River Turtle, *Carettochelys insculpta*
RANGE: New Guinea: Fly River area
HABITAT: rivers
SIZE: 46 cm (18 in)

This New Guinea species, now also discovered to be living in northern Australia, is better adapted for aquatic life than most freshwater turtles. Its limbs are modified into long paddles but retain two claws and resemble the limbs of sea turtles. There are few details about the nesting habits of this species, but it lays 17 to 27 eggs and the hatchlings are about 6 cm (2¼ in) long.

PLATYSTERNIDAE: Big-headed Turtle Family

The single living species in this family is a freshwater turtle found in Southeast Asia.

NAME: Big-headed Turtle, *Platysternon megacephalum*
RANGE: Burma, Thailand, S. China
HABITAT: mountain streams, rivers
SIZE: 15–18 cm (6–7 in)

Although a relatively small species in carapace length, this turtle has a huge head, almost half the width of the carapace. The head is not retractile and the carapace is slightly shaped to allow the head and the short, thick neck to be raised. The feet of this turtle are small and only partially webbed, and there are enlarged, flattened scales on the forelimbs.

The big-headed turtle is an unusually agile climber and, using its outstretched claws, it clambers over branches and rocks in search of food or a basking spot. It lays only 2 eggs at a time.

DERMATEMYIDAE: Central American River Turtle Family

A single species survives from this once widespread family, formerly found in North and Central America, Europe and Africa.

NAME: Central American River Turtle, *Dermatemys mawi*
RANGE: Mexico to Guatemala and Belize (not Yucatán)
HABITAT: clear rivers and lakes
SIZE: 46 cm (18 in) ⓥ

This turtle has long been hunted for its meat and is now scarce throughout much of its range. Although protected to some degree by conservation laws, there is still concern for its future.

A smooth-shelled turtle, it has a relatively small head with a pointed, projecting snout and large nostrils. Males have a golden-yellow patch on the head, but the females and juveniles have greyish heads. It has large webbed feet and is one of the most aquatic of all freshwater turtles; it rarely climbs out on the bank to bask but floats on the water instead. On land this turtle is awkward, but it swims well and is able to stay submerged for long periods. Aquatic vegetation is its main food source. It nests in the flood season and lays its 6 to 16 eggs in mud near the water's edge.

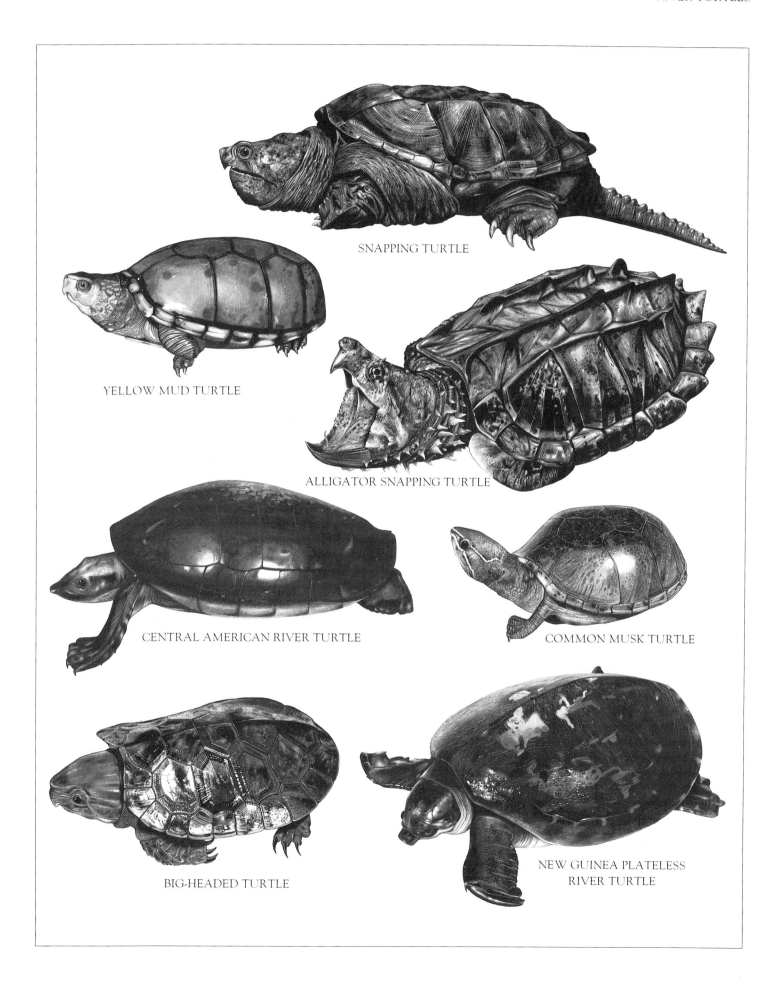

SNAPPING TURTLE

YELLOW MUD TURTLE

ALLIGATOR SNAPPING TURTLE

CENTRAL AMERICAN RIVER TURTLE

COMMON MUSK TURTLE

BIG-HEADED TURTLE

NEW GUINEA PLATELESS
RIVER TURTLE

Leatherback, Marine Turtles

DERMOCHELYIDAE:
Leatherback Family

There is a single living species in this family. It has many distinctive features but resembles other sea turtles in many details of skull structure and has similar nesting habits.

NAME: Leatherback, *Dermochelys coriacea*
RANGE: world-wide, usually in warm seas
HABITAT: oceanic
SIZE: 155 cm (61 in)   (E)

The world's largest turtle, the leatherback has an average weight of 360 kg (800 lb) and a maximum of 590 kg (1,300 lb). Its foreflippers are extremely long, with a span of about 2.7 m (9 ft). It has no horny shields on its shell, no scales and no claws. The carapace resembles hard rubber and has three longitudinal ridges. Leatherbacks feed mainly on jellyfish, a diet in keeping with their weak, scissorlike jaws.

Leatherbacks apparently perform long migrations between nesting and feeding sites. Most breed every other year and lay clutches of about 80 to 100 eggs. The nesting procedure is much the same as that of the other sea turtles, but, after laying, the leatherback always turns one or more circles before returning to the sea. Several clutches are laid in a season at roughly 10-day intervals. Hatchlings are 6 cm (2¼ in) long and have scales on shell and skin which disappear within the first 2 months of life.

CHELONIDAE:
Marine Turtle Family

The larger of the 2 families of marine turtles, Chelonidae contains 6 species, all generally found in tropical and subtropical waters. All have non-retractile heads and limbs. The forelimbs are modified into long, paddlelike flippers with one or two claws; the turtles swim by making winglike beats of the foreflippers. On land, the green turtle moves particularly awkwardly, heaving itself forward with both flippers simultaneously, but the others move with alternating movements of the limbs, as most four-legged animals do.

The 6 species have become specialized for different niches and diets, to compensate for the inevitable overlap of their ranges in many oceans.

NAME: Green Turtle, *Chelonia mydas*
RANGE: world-wide in seas where temperature does not fall below 20°C (68°F)
HABITAT: coasts, open sea
SIZE: 102–127 cm (40–50 in)   (E)

This large, thoroughly aquatic turtle rarely comes to land except to bask and sleep and to lay eggs. Males have slightly longer, narrower carapaces than females and enlarged curved claws on the front flippers for gripping the female when mating.

Green turtles are primarily herbivorous animals and have serrated jaw surfaces, well suited to feeding on sea grasses and seaweed; some crustaceans and jellyfish may also be eaten. The best feeding grounds, where there are vast underwater pastures of plants, are often far away from the best nesting beaches, and green turtles have evolved astounding migratory habits. At nesting time they travel hundreds of miles to the beach of their birth to lay eggs and, as a result, there tend to be a limited number of important nesting sites, to which hundreds of turtles go. One such site is Ascension Island in the mid-Atlantic.

Every second or third year, green turtles travel to their nesting site and mate. The female heaves herself up the beach well away from the tidal area. With her foreflippers she sweeps away sand to create a hollow for her body in which she lies, her shell flush with the beach. She then uses her hind flippers to dig a hole about 40 cm (16 in) deep, immediately beneath her tail. She deposits her eggs into the hole, covers the area with sand and returns to the sea. The average clutch contains about 106 eggs. Sometimes a female lays several clutches in a season at 2-week intervals.

After a 2- to 3-month incubation period, the young turtles hatch and dig their way through the sand to the surface. Having oriented themselves, they rush for the sea, past a horde of eager predators. Mortality is high, and those which do reach the sea will have to face yet more predators.

The green turtle is now an endangered species, and the population has been eliminated in some areas although it is still reasonable in others. The turtles have been over-exploited for their meat, hides and eggs, and the predictability of their nesting habits has made them easy victims. Exploitation is now strictly controlled, and imports banned in many countries.

The closely related flatback turtle, *C. depressa*, is a little smaller than the green turtle and lives off the coast of Northern Australia.

NAME: Loggerhead Turtle, *Caretta caretta*
RANGE: temperate and tropical areas of the Pacific, Indian and Atlantic Oceans
HABITAT: coasts, open sea
SIZE: 76–102 cm (30–40 in)   (V)

A large turtle with a long, slightly tapering carapace, the loggerhead has a wide chunky head housing powerful jaws. It can crush even hard-shelled prey and feeds on crabs and molluscs as well as on sponges, jellyfish and aquatic plants.

Loggerheads usually breed every other year and lay three or four clutches of about 100 eggs each in a season.

The loggerhead population has been reduced by over-collection of eggs and lack of hunting controls, but in southeast Africa, where the turtles have been protected for more than 10 years, their numbers have increased by over 50 per cent.

NAME: Pacific Ridley, *Lepidochelys olivacea*
RANGE: tropical Pacific, Indian and S. Atlantic Oceans
HABITAT: coasts, open sea
SIZE: 66 cm (26 in)   (E)

The Pacific ridley is small and lightly built for a sea turtle. It feeds on small shrimp, jellyfish, crabs, snails and fish, which it crushes with strong jaws. Like its close relative Kemp's ridley, *L. kempi*, the Pacific ridley breeds every year and always returns to the same nesting beaches. The female lays about 100 eggs in a pit in the sand and covers them. She then begins a strange movement peculiar to ridleys, rocking from side to side so that each edge of the shell thumps the sand in turn. Both ridleys are in grave danger due to over-exploitation by man.

NAME: Hawksbill, *Eretmochelys imbricata*
RANGE: tropical Atlantic, Pacific and Indian Oceans; Caribbean
HABITAT: coral reefs, rocky coasts
SIZE: 76–91 cm (30–36 in)   (E)

The hawksbill's beautiful carapace provides the best tortoise-shell and is the reason for the endangered status of the species. Conservation controls have been introduced after many years of hunting, and imports banned in some countries. The carapace is serrated at the back and has particularly thick horny plates. The tapering head of the hawksbill is an adaptation for searching out food, such as molluscs and crustaceans, in rocky crevices and reefs.

In many areas hawksbills are opportunistic breeders, nesting on any beach convenient to feeding grounds. They lay more eggs at a time than any other turtle, usually about 150.

LEATHERBACK

GREEN TURTLE

HAWKSBILL

PACIFIC RIDLEY

LOGGERHEAD TURTLE

Softshell Turtles, Greaved Turtles, Matamatas

TRIONYCHIDAE: Softshell Turtle Family

This family contains 32 species of aquatic turtles which have only three claws on each foot. All species have rounded, flexible carapaces with no horny plates, hence their pancakelike appearance and their common name. Most species have long mobile necks. Softshells move fast in water and on land but spend most of their lives in water. Species are found in eastern North America and Southeast Asia, and there is a single species in the Middle East.

Softshells lay up to three clutches of hard-shelled eggs each year. Females usually grow larger than males and, as they mature, their carapace patterns become obscured by blotches. Males tend to retain clear carapace patterns.

NAME: **Spiny Softshell**, *Trionyx spiniferus*
RANGE: **N. America: Ontario and Quebec, south to Florida and Colorado**
HABITAT: **rivers, creeks, ponds**
SIZE: **15–46 cm (6–18 in)**

Conical projections, or tubercles, around the front edge of this turtle's shell are the origin of its common name. There are about six geographically distinct races and some have more pronounced spines than others. Females are notably larger than males.

Spiny softshells are highly aquatic; they feed on insects, crayfish, and some fish and plant food. They nest in summer and lay about 20 eggs.

NAME: **Narrow-headed/Indian Softshell**, *Chitra indica*
RANGE: **India, Pakistan, Thailand**
HABITAT: **rivers**
SIZE: **91 cm (36 in)**

A large, fast-swimming turtle with flipperlike limbs, this softshell does indeed have an elongated narrow head, with eyes placed far forward near the snout. It seems to prefer clear, sandy-bottomed water and is carnivorous, feeding in the main on fish and molluscs.

NAME: **Nile Softshell**, *Trionyx triunguis*
RANGE: **Africa: Egypt to Senegal**
HABITAT: **ponds, lakes, rivers**
SIZE: **91 cm (36 in)**

The Nile softshell can weigh up to 45 kg (100 lb) and is hunted for food by man in many parts of its range. Although it is a freshwater species, groups have been found living off the coast of Turkey. It is omnivorous and feeds on molluscs, fish, insects and fruit. In Egypt it breeds in April and lays 50 to 60 eggs; elsewhere clutches may be smaller.

NAME: **Zambesi Softshell**, *Cycloderma frenatum*
RANGE: **Africa: Tanzania, Mozambique, Zambia, Malawi**
HABITAT: **ponds, lakes, rivers**
SIZE: **51 cm (20 in)**

A carnivorous turtle, the Zambesi softshell feeds mainly on molluscs. It lays its 15 to 20 eggs from December to March and is most active in rainy weather. Hatchlings have pale green carapaces and dark lines on their heads. In adults these lines are outlined with white dots and become fainter with age. The only other species in this genus is Aubry's softshell, *C. Aubry*, found in West Africa.

PELOMEDUSIDAE: Greaved Turtle Family

This family of 19 species is one of the 2 families of side-neck turtles. A side-neck retracts its head by moving it sideways under the carapace. This leaves an undefended area of the head and neck exposed, and may have prevented the evolution of any terrestrial side-necks, since they would be too vulnerable to mammalian predators. All these turtles live in fresh water in Africa, Madagascar and South America, east of the Andes.

NAME: **Arrau River Turtle**, *Podocnemis expansa*
RANGE: **northern South America**
HABITAT: **Orinoco and Amazon river systems**
SIZE: **61–76 cm (24–30 in)**   Ⓔ

The largest of the side-necks, the Arrau turtle may weigh over 45 kg (100 lb). Females have wide, flattened shells and are larger and more numerous than males. Adults feed entirely on plant food.

The nesting habits of these turtles are similar to those of sea turtles in that they gather in large numbers to travel to certain suitable nesting areas. They lay their eggs on sandbanks which are exposed only in the dry season, and there are relatively few such sites. The females come out on to the sandbanks at night and each lays as many as 90 or 100 softshelled eggs. They then return to their feeding grounds. The hatchlings, which are about 5 cm (2 in) long, emerge to the attentions of many predators; even without man's activities, only about 5 per cent reach adult feeding grounds.

Uncontrolled hunting of adults and excessive collecting of eggs have seriously reduced the population of this turtle. It is now an endangered species and is protected in most areas.

CHELIDAE: Matamata and Snake-necked Turtle Family

The other family of side-neck turtles contains 30 species, found in South America, Australia and New Guinea. This family shows a number of structural advancements over the more primitive Pelomedusids. They are carnivorous animals and live in rivers and marshes.

NAME: **Matamata**, *Chelus fimbriatus*
RANGE: **northern South America**
HABITAT: **rivers**
SIZE: **41 cm (16 in)**

The matamata is one of the most bizarre of all turtles. Its carapace is exceedingly rough and ridged and, from above, its head is flat and virtually triangular. Its eyes are tiny and positioned close to the thin, tubelike snout. Fleshy flaps at the sides of the head wave in the water, possibly attracting small fishes. The matamata's neck is thick and muscular and its actual mouth extremely wide. Its limbs are small and weak.

Well camouflaged by its irregular outline, the matamata lies at the bottom of the water. It is so sedentary that algae grow on its shell, adding to the camouflage. When a fish swims by, it opens its huge mouth, sucking in both water and fish. The turtle then closes its mouth, leaving only a slit for the water to flow out, and swallows the fish.

Matamatas lay 12 to 28 eggs; the young have light-tan-coloured carapaces.

NAME: **Murray River Turtle**, *Emydura macquarri*
RANGE: **S.E. Australia**
HABITAT: **rivers**
SIZE: **30 cm (11¾ in)**

The Murray River turtle is a well-known Australian side-neck. The shape of its carapace alters with age: hatchlings have almost circular carapaces; in juveniles, carapaces are widest at the back; and adults have virtually oval shells. The head of the Murray River turtle is quite small, with bright eyes and a light band extending back from the mouth. It is an active species and feeds on frogs, tadpoles and vegetation. In summer it lays 10 to 15 eggs in a chamber dug in the river bank. These normally hatch in 10 or 11 weeks.

SPINY SOFTSHELL

NARROW-HEADED SOFTSHELL

NILE SOFTSHELL

ZAMBESI SOFTSHELL

MATAMATA

ARRAU RIVER TURTLE

MURRAY RIVER TURTLE

Crocodiles, Alligators and Caimans, Gavial

NAME: **Gavial**, *Gavialis gangeticus*
RANGE: **N. India**
HABITAT: **large rivers**
SIZE: **7 m (23 ft)**　Ⓔ

The Indian gavial has an extremely long narrow snout, studded with about 100 small teeth — ideal equipment for seizing fish and frogs under water. Like all crocodilians, the gavial has been hunted for its skin and it is now one of the rarest in Asia. Its hind limbs are paddlelike, and the gavial seems rarely to leave the water except to nest. The female lays her eggs at night in a pit dug in the river bank.

NAME: **American Alligator**, *Alligator mississipiensis* (sic)
RANGE: **S. E. USA**
HABITAT: **marshes, rivers, swamps**
SIZE: **up to 5.5 m (18 ft)**　Ⓞ

The American alligator, once struggling for survival against hunters and habitat destruction, has been so effectively protected by conservation laws that the population is now on the increase.

These alligators usually mate in shallow water in April, and courtship is slow and quiet. The male stays with the female for several days before mating, occasionally stroking her body with his forelimbs. As she nears acquiescence, he rubs her throat with his head and blows bubbles past her cheeks. The female finds a nest site near water and scrapes up whatever plant debris is available with sweeping movements of her body and tail. She packs the vegetation together to form a mound, with a cavity for the eggs. She lays 28 to 52 eggs and crawls over the mound to close the cavity with more vegetation. She guards the nest while the eggs incubate for about 65 days. The hatching young call out to their mother, prompting her to open the nest and free them. They remain with her for up to 3 years.

NAME: **Spectacled Caiman**, *Caiman crocodilus*
RANGE: **Venezuela to S. Amazon basin**
HABITAT: **slow still waters, lakes, swamps**
SIZE: **1.5–2 m (5–6½ ft) long**　Ⓔ

There are several species and subspecies of this caiman and its name has been the subject of much dispute; it is often known as *C. sclerops*. Its common name derives from the ridge on the head between the eyes which resembles the bridge of a pair of spectacles. The population of wild caimans has declined drastically since they are not only hunted for skins but the young are also collected and sold as pets or stuffed as curios. The female caiman makes a nest of plant debris scraped together into a pile and lays an average of 30 eggs.

ORDER CROCODILIA

The crocodiles, alligators and caimans and the single species of gavial are the 3 families which together make up this order and include the largest and most dangerous living reptiles. All are powerful amphibious carnivores, preying on a range of vertebrate animals, although juvenile crocodiles also eat insects and other small invertebrates. The crocodilia are the most direct evolutionary descendants of the archosaurs, the dominant animal life-forms from the Triassac to the end of the Cretaceous eras (190 to 65 million years ago). There are about 21 species alive today: 13 in the crocodile family, 7 alligators and caimans, and 1 gavial. All are found in tropical and subtropical regions. Males and females look alike in all species and it is difficult to determine the sex visually. Males do tend to grow larger than females.

All members of the order have elongate short-limbed bodies, covered with horny skin scales. Thickened bony plates on the back give added protection. The crocodilian's predatory armament is a long snout with many conical teeth anchored in deep sockets in the jaw bones. Breathing organs are highly modified for underwater predation: the external nostrils, on a projection at the snout-tip, have valves to close them off, while a pair of flaps in the throat forms another valve which enables the animal to hold prey in its open jaws beneath the surface, without inhaling water.

Both crocodiles and alligators possess a pair of large teeth near the front of the lower jaw for grasping prey. In the crocodiles, these two teeth fit into distinct notches in the upper jaw and are visible when the jaws are closed, while in the alligators, the large teeth are accommodated in bony pits in the upper jaw.

NAME: **West African Dwarf Crocodile**, *Osteolaemus tetraspis*
RANGE: **W. Africa, south of the Sahara**
HABITAT: **streams and lakes**
SIZE: **1.5 m (5 ft)**　Ⓔ

Also known as the short-nosed crocodile, this animal is indeed characterized by its unusually short snout. It is now extremely rare owing to over-exploitation for skins and to the destruction of its habitat. It resembles the New World alligators in appearance and size, although it is a member of the crocodile family. Little is known of its biology and breeding habits.

NAME: **Estuarine Crocodile**, *Crocodylus porosus*
RANGE: **S. India through Indonesia; S. Australia**
HABITAT: **estuaries, coasts, mangroves**
SIZE: **up to 6 m (19½ ft)**　Ⓥ

The estuarine crocodile is one of the largest and most dangerous species and has been known to attack man. It is rapidly being exterminated since its hide is considered the most valuable of all crocodiles' for leather, and its large size makes the hunt well worth while. It is now illegal to catch the estuarine crocodile in many areas, but the population is still low. Where hunting is allowed, it is restricted, and skin exports are controlled.

The most aquatic and most marine of all crocodile species, the estuarine crocodile spends little time on land and swims great distances. The female lays 25 to 90 eggs in a mound of plant debris which she scrapes together near water. She guards the eggs for about 3 months while they incubate.

NAME: **Nile Crocodile**, *Crocodylus niloticus*
RANGE: **Africa (not Sahara or N. West)**
HABITAT: **large rivers, lakes, marshes**
SIZE: **4.5–5 m (15–16½ ft) long**　Ⓔ

The population and range of the once widespread Nile crocodile is now seriously reduced, by both the demand for skins and the destruction of natural habitats. The Nile crocodile preys on large mammals and birds which come to the water's edge to drink. After seizing its catch, the crocodile drowns it by holding it under water, and then twists off chunks of flesh by spinning its own body in the water while holding on to the prey. Adult crocodiles swallow stones, which remain in the stomach and act as stabilizing ballast when the crocodiles are in water.

The Nile crocodile spends its nights in water and comes out on to land just before sunrise in order to bask in the sun during the day. It leads a rather leisurely existence and does not need to feed every day.

The male defends a territory and enacts a courtship display at breeding time. The mated female lays 25 to 75 eggs in a pit near the water. She covers her eggs well and guards them during the 3-month incubation period. When ready to hatch, the young are sensitive to the footfalls of their mother overhead. They call to her from the nest; she uncovers them and carries them inside her mouth to a safe nursery area, where she cares for them assiduously for another 3 to 6 months. The young feed on insects, then progress to crabs, birds and fish before adopting the adult diet.

SPECTACLED CAIMAN

NILE CROCODILE

ESTUARINE CROCODILE

WEST AFRICAN DWARF CROCODILE

GAVIAL

AMERICAN ALLIGATOR

Tuatara, Iguanas I

ORDER RHYNCHOCEPHALIA

Apart from a single species, the tuatara, living in New Zealand, this order of reptiles is known only from fossils.

SPHENODONTIA: Tuatara Family

The sole family in the Rhynchocephalia order contains only 1 species, which is believed to be extremely similar to related species alive 130 million years ago. The scientific name means "the wedge-toothed ones" and refers to the sharp teeth, fused into both jawbones.

NAME: Tuatara, *Sphenodon punctatus*
RANGE: New Zealand
HABITAT: woods with little undergrowth
SIZE: up to 65 cm (25½ in) Ⓞ

A powerfully built reptile, the tuatara has a large head and a crest running from its head down its back. The male is generally larger than the female. Active at dusk and at night, the tuatara has the least need of warmth of any reptile — it is quite content at 12° C (53° F) whereas most reptiles prefer over 25° C (77° F). Its metabolism and growth rate are correspondingly slow. Tuataras are ground-living and shelter in burrows which they dig in loose soil or take over from shearwaters. They feed on crickets, earthworms, snails, young birds and lizards.

The female tuatara lays up to 15 eggs in a hole she digs in the soil. They hatch 13 to 15 months later — the longest development time of any reptile. She probably does not breed every year. Tuataras are long-lived and probably do not attain sexual maturity until they are about 20 years old. Once in danger of extinction from introduced predators, healthy tuatara populations now live in special island sanctuaries and are protected by conservation laws.

ORDER SQUAMATA

The largest reptilian order, the Squamata includes all the lizards, snakes and amphisbaenids — more than 6,000 species in all.

IGUANIDAE: Iguana Family

There are more than 600 species in this family, the vast majority of which live in the Americas, although there are a few species in Madagascar and Fiji. They are the New World equivalents of the Old World agamid lizards and nowhere do the two families occur together.

Most iguanas are ground- or tree-living and feed on insects and small invertebrates. Many are brightly coloured and perform elaborate courtship displays.

NAME: Common Iguana, *Iguana iguana*
RANGE: Central and N. South America; introduced in USA: Florida
HABITAT: forest, trees near water
SIZE: 1–2 m (3¼–6½ ft)

The common iguana has a characteristic crest of comblike spines, longest at the neck area but running all the way down its body and tail. The bands across the shoulders and tail become darker as the iguana gets older — juveniles are bright green. Active in the daytime, these iguanas are agile tree-dwelling lizards which also swim readily. They are herbivores but will defend themselves with their sharp teeth and claws when they are attacked.

In autumn, the female lays 28 to 40 eggs in a hole she digs in the ground. The eggs hatch in about 3 months.

NAME: Eastern Fence Lizard, *Sceloporus undulatus*
RANGE: USA: Virginia to Florida, west to New Mexico; Mexico
HABITAT: open woodland, grassland
SIZE: 9–20 cm (3½–7¾ in)

This iguana occurs in many subspecies, with varying coloration over its range, but it always has a characteristic roughened surface because of its keeled scales. Either arboreal or terrestrial, depending on its habitat, it is active during the day and feeds on most insects, particularly beetles, as well as spiders, centipedes and snails.

The courting male holds a territory which he vigorously defends against competitors while he attracts his mate. The female lays 3 to 12 eggs under a log or other debris and may produce up to four clutches a season.

NAME: Chuckwalla, *Sauromalus obesus*
RANGE: USA: S. California, Nevada, Utah, Arizona; Mexico
HABITAT: rocky desert
SIZE: 28–42 cm (11–16½ in)

A dark-skinned, plump-bodied lizard, the chuckwalla has a thick, pale yellow tail with a blunt tip. The male tends to be darker than the female, with some red or yellow speckling on the body, while females and juveniles often have dark crossbands. The chuckwalla hides under a rock or in a crevice during the night and emerges in the morning to bask in the sun and warm its body. An herbivorous lizard, it then searches for leaves, buds and flowers to eat, often feeding on the creosote bush.

The chuckwalla is well adapted for desert life: in the folds of skin on its sides are accessory lymph glands in which it can store liquid, when it is available, for use in prolonged dry seasons. The female is thought to breed every other year and lays 5 to 10 eggs at a time.

NAME: Green Anole, *Anolis carolinensis*
RANGE: USA: Virginia to Florida, west to Texas
HABITAT: forest edge, roadsides
SIZE: 12–20 cm (4¼–7¾ in)

The green anole has a slender body and long toe pads as an adaptation for its tree-dwelling habits. Although usually green, it can turn brown in seconds. It is active during the day and feeds on insects and spiders.

The remarkable pink, fanlike flap on the throat of the male is used in courtship display. His display triggers sexual receptivity and ovulation in the female. She lays her eggs, one at a time, at 2-week intervals throughout the breeding season, from April to September. The eggs hatch in 5 to 7 weeks.

NAME: Collared Lizard, *Crotaphytus collaris*
RANGE: USA: Utah, Colorado, south to Texas; Mexico
HABITAT: rocky hillsides, forest
SIZE: 20–35.5 cm (7¾–14 in)

The robust collared lizard has a large head and a distinctive collar of dark and light markings. Active in the daytime, it particularly likes to bask around rocks where there are crevices for refuge. It feeds on insects and small lizards.

The female collared lizard lays up to 12 eggs in midsummer. The young, measuring about 9 cm (3½ in), hatch 2 to 3 months later.

NAME: Texas Horned Lizard, *Phrynosoma cornutum*
RANGE: USA: Kansas to Texas, Arizona; introduced in Florida
HABITAT: arid country
SIZE: 6–18 cm (2¼–7 in)

The well-armoured Texas horned lizard has a flattened body with pointed scales fringing each side. Behind its head are two enlarged horns, flanked by enlarged scales. In its arid habitat, it may bury itself under loose soil or seek refuge under bushes. It feeds largely on ants.

The female lizard digs a hole in which she lays her 14 to 36 eggs in midsummer; the eggs hatch in about 6 weeks.

NAME: Forest Iguana, *Polychrus gutterosus*
RANGE: tropical South America
HABITAT: forest
SIZE: up to 50 cm (19¾ in) including tail of up to 37 cm (14½ in)

A tree-dwelling iguana, this long-legged lizard lies on a branch, its flattened body pressed inconspicuously to the surface, waiting for insect prey. It is a good climber, able to hold on to a branch with its hind legs alone, but it is slow-moving.

The female forest iguana lays clutches of 7 or 8 eggs.

GREEN ANOLE (male)

FOREST IGUANA

COMMON IGUANA

CHUCKWALLA (male)

COLLARED LIZARD

EASTERN FENCE LIZARD

TUATARA

TEXAS HORNED LIZARD

Iguanas 2

NAME: **Marine Iguana,** *Amblyrhynchus cristatus*
RANGE: **Galápagos Islands**
HABITAT: **lava rocks on coasts**
SIZE: **1.2–1.5 m (4–5 ft)** (R)

The only present-day lizard to use the sea as a major habitat, the marine iguana swims and dives readily as it forages for seaweed, its main food. Vital adaptations to marine life are the nasal glands that remove the excess salt the iguana takes in with its food; the salt is expelled in a thin shower of water vapour which the iguana blows out through its nose. When swimming, the iguana uses its powerful tail for propulsion; its feet are normally held against the body, but they are sometimes used to steer a course. The iguana cannot breathe under water, but when it dives, its heart rate slows down, reducing the blood flow through the body and thus conserving the limited supplies of oxygen.

Male marine iguanas are highly territorial and fight to defend their own small areas of breeding territory on the shore. The combat is ritualistic, each individual trying to overthrow the other by butting him with his head. In one race of marine iguanas, breeding males develop green crests and red flanks. After mating, the female finds a sandy area in which to bury her eggs. She digs a hole about 30.5 cm (12 in) deep, lays 2 or 3 eggs and covers them with sand. The eggs incubate for about 112 days.

Numbers of these once abundant creatures have been reduced by predators, introduced by settlers and sailors. Previously there were no native mammalian predators to threaten their existence.

NAME: **Galápagos Land Iguana,** *Conolophus subcristatus*
RANGE: **Galápagos Islands**
HABITAT: **arid land, coasts to volcanoes**
SIZE: **up to 1.2 m (4 ft)** (V)

Once common on all of the Galápagos islands, this iguana is now extinct in some and rare in others. Many have been shot for food or sport, and others have suffered from the ravages of introduced predators. Conservation measures have now been established.

A stout-bodied animal with a rounded tail, the land iguana is generally yellow or brown, sometimes with irregular spots on the body. It has a crest at the back of the neck, and older individuals have rolls of fat around the neck. It lives in arid land where there is some vegetation and where it can dig into the soil to make a burrow for shelter. Plants, including cacti, are its main food; it may also eat some small animals. Breeding females lay clutches of about 9 eggs.

NAME: **Basilisk Lizard,** *Basiliscus plumifrons*
RANGE: **South America**
HABITAT: **forest**
SIZE: **80 cm (31½ in)**

Male basilisk lizards sport prominent, impressive crests on back and tail and bony casques on the head. The 5 species in the genus are all extremely alike and can be distinguished only by the characteristic shapes of the head casques of the males; these casques are poorly developed in females and absent in juveniles.

The long-legged basilisks are among the few four-legged animals to run on two legs. They rear up on their hind legs and run in a semi-erect position, with the long tail held up to help balance. This counterweighting effect is vital and if too much of the tail is amputated the iguana is unable to rise up on its hind legs. Adults have achieved speeds of 11 km/h (6.8 mph) but only over short distances. Basilisks can even run a few yards over smooth water, held up by the surface film, and then swim when it is no longer possible for them to remain on the surface.

Active in the daytime, basilisks feed on fruit and small animals, often climbing into trees to find food. In the breeding season, females lay 10 to 15 eggs which incubate for about 80 days.

NAME: **Rhinoceros Iguana,** *Cyclura cornuta*
RANGE: **Haiti and other islands of the Lesser Antilles**
HABITAT: **arid scrub**
SIZE: **up to 1.2 m (4 ft)** (V)

The male rhinoceros iguana is easily identified by the characteristic protuberances on the tip of his snout that are formed from enlarged scales. The female has only small, inconspicuous protuberances. A large, powerful species, this iguana has a strong tail and a somewhat compressed body. Some individuals, particularly old males, develop rolls of fat at the back of the head. There are many races of rhinoceros iguana with only minor physical variations. They are among the most primitive iguanas.

Rhinoceros iguanas live on land, among thorn bushes and cacti, and feed on plants, worms and mice. Breeding females lay clutches of about 12 eggs which incubate for 120 days or more. In some islands of the Lesser Antilles this iguana has been displaced by the common iguana which has recently become established.

NAME: **Spiny-tailed Iguana,** *Ctenosaura pectinata*
RANGE: **Mexico, Central America**
HABITAT: **forest**
SIZE: **1 m (3¼ ft)**

A land-dwelling lizard, the spiny-tailed iguana is so called because its tail is ringed with spiny scales, making it an effective weapon. These iguanas feed mainly on plant material, particularly on beans, but also catch some small animals. Their diet is rich in potassium salts, and they are equipped with nasal glands to excrete excess salt, which then collects as encrustations round the nostrils.

Highly gregarious and territorial, these iguanas live in colonies, ruled by a strict pecking order. One male in the colony is dominant and, although the other males hold territories, they will only defend them against one another and not against the leader. In the breeding season, females dig burrows in which to lay their clutches of about 50 eggs.

NAME: **Fijian Banded Iguana,** *Brachylophus fasciatus*
RANGE: **islands of Fiji and Tonga**
HABITAT: **woodland, forest**
SIZE: **90 cm (35½ in)** (E)

One of the few iguana species found outside the Americas, the Fijian iguana has an extremely long tail, often more than twice the length of its slender body, and a low crest along its back. An arboreal iguana, its elongate fingers and toes are equipped with sharp claws for climbing. The female has a uniformly green body, while the male is banded with lighter green and has light spots on his neck. They feed on leaves and other plant material.

The Fijian iguana is a little-known species that may be nearing extinction because of the destruction of much of its forest habitat and the introduction into its range of mongooses, which prey on the iguana and its eggs.

NAME: **Madagascan Iguana,** *Oplurus* **sp.**
RANGE: **Madagascar, small offshore islands**
HABITAT: **forest**
SIZE: **up to 38 cm (15 in)**

There are 2 iguana genera in Madagascar: *Oplurus* and *Chalarodon*. The 6 species of *Oplurus* are all similar in appearance, with rings of spiny scales on their tapering tails. *Chalarodon* species are easily distinguished by their small crests, which *Oplurus* species lack, and their smooth-scaled tails.

Primarily land-dwelling, these iguanas can climb and often take refuge in bushes and trees.

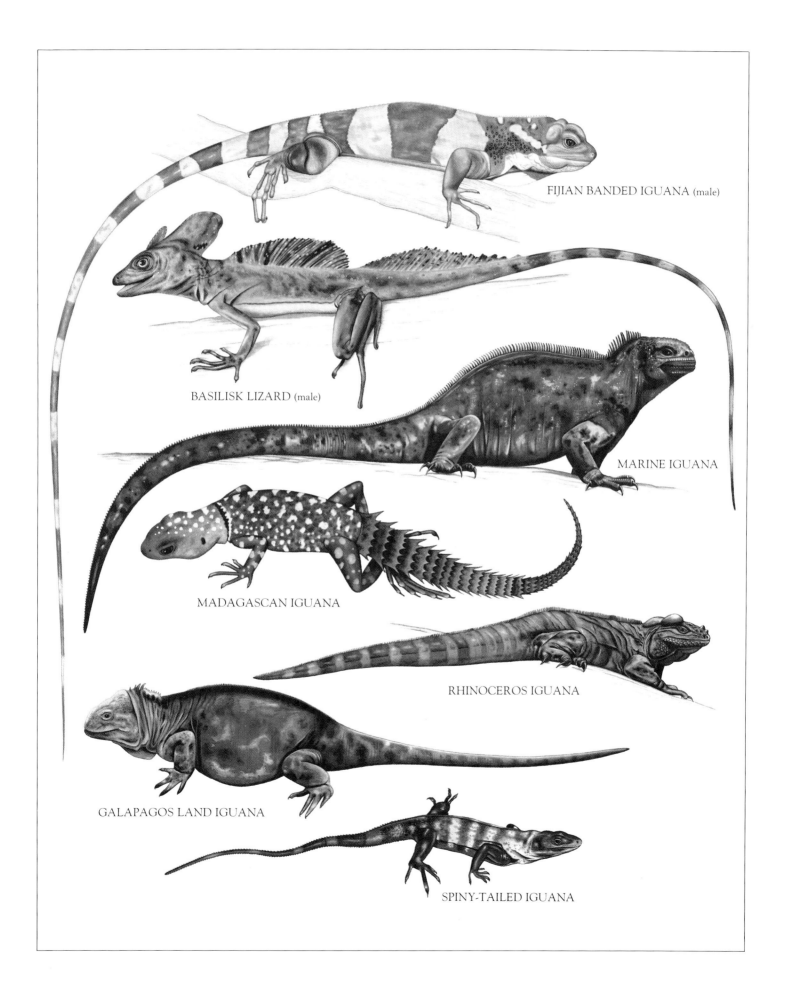

FIJIAN BANDED IGUANA (male)

BASILISK LIZARD (male)

MARINE IGUANA

MADAGASCAN IGUANA

RHINOCEROS IGUANA

GALAPAGOS LAND IGUANA

SPINY-TAILED IGUANA

Agamid Lizards

NAME: **Common Agama,** *Agama agama*
RANGE: **central Africa**
HABITAT: **tropical forest**
SIZE: **12 cm (4¾ in)**

Agamas live in groups of 2 to 25 in a defined territory, ruled by one dominant male. They are active during the day, emerging at dawn to bask in the sun and feed, mainly on insects. If the dominant male is challenged by another male, he adopts a threat posture, bobbing his head, raising his body off the ground and spreading the folds of his neck skin as far as possible.

Mating usually coincides with the rainy season, when the earth is sufficiently moist for the female agamid to make her nest. She digs a small hole in damp soil in which she lays 4 to 6 eggs. She covers the eggs over and smooths the ground surface to conceal the nest. While they develop, the eggs absorb moisture from the soil. The young hatch in 2 or 3 months.

NAME: **Flying Dragon,** *Draco volans*
RANGE: **Philippines to Malaysia and Indonesia**
HABITAT: **rain forest, rubber plantations**
SIZE: **19–22 cm (7½–8½ in)**

An arboreal lizard, the so-called flying dragon actually glides from tree to tree on winglike skin flaps. At each side of its body, between front and hind limbs, there is a large flap of skin supported by extended movable ribs. Usually these flaps are held folded at the sides of the body, but they can be extended to carry the lizard in an almost horizontal glide for many metres. The flying dragon feeds on insects, particularly ants.

To breed, the flying dragon descends to the ground and buries its 1 to 4 eggs in the soil.

NAME: **Frilled Lizard,** *Chlamydosaurus kingii*
RANGE: **Australia: N. Western Australia, N. Northern Territory, E. Queensland; New Guinea**
HABITAT: **dry forest, woodland**
SIZE: **66 cm (26 in) including tail of 44 cm (17¼ in)**

This slender, long-tailed lizard has an extraordinary rufflike collar of skin around its neck which may be as much as 25.5 cm (10 in) in diameter. Normally this collar lies in folds around the neck and shoulders but, if alarmed, the lizard opens its mouth wide and at the same time the brightly coloured frill erects, giving the animal a startling appearance and making it look larger than it really is in order to intimidate the enemy.

Active in the daytime, the frilled lizard forages in trees and on the ground for insects and other small animals.

AGAMIDAE:
Agamid Lizard Family

The agamid family contains more than 300 species of plump-bodied lizards, found throughout the warmer regions of the Old World except in Madagascar and New Zealand.

Most agamids have thin tails, long legs and triangular-shaped heads. They live on the ground, in trees or among rocks and feed mainly on insects and other small invertebrates, but also on some plant matter.

NAME: **Thorny Devil,** *Moloch horridus*
RANGE: **Australia: Western, North and South, Queensland**
HABITAT: **arid scrub, desert**
SIZE: **16 cm (6¼ in)**

The grotesque thorny devil is the only species in its genus and one of the strangest of lizards. Its body bristles with large, conical spines, and it has spines above each eye and a spiny hump behind its head. The tail, too, is spiny. It is a slow-moving creature which forages for its food, mainly ants and termites, on the ground.

The female thorny devil lays 3 to 10 eggs, usually 8, in November or December. The newly hatched young are tiny, spiny replicas of their parents.

NAME: **Princely Mastigure,** *Uromastyx princeps*
RANGE: **Africa: Somali Republic**
HABITAT: **rocky, stony land**
SIZE: **about 23 cm (9 in)**

A plump-bodied lizard, the princely mastigure has a short, thick tail, studded with large spines, and a small turtlelike head. It is active by day, sheltering at night in holes or crevices in the rocks. Grass, flowers, fruit and leaves are its main foods. If attacked, it defends itself against the enemy with its spiny tail, lashing it to and fro.

NAME: **Arabian Toad-headed Agamid,** *Phrynocephalus nejdensis*
RANGE: **S.W. Asia**
HABITAT: **desert, semi-desert**
SIZE: **up to 12.5 cm (5 in)**

The Arabian toad-headed agamid has a rounded head, long slender legs and a tapering tail. It is a burrowing lizard and digs short tunnels for shelter; it also buries itself in sand by wriggling from side to side. If alarmed it adopts a defence posture, with tail raised, and then rolls and unrolls its tail. It feeds mainly on insects and also eats some flowers, fruit and leaves.

Females lay several clutches of eggs during the year.

NAME: **Bearded Dragon,** *Amphibolurus barbatus*
RANGE: **Australia: E. and S. E. (except Cape York Peninsula and Tasmania)**
HABITAT: **arid land to forest**
SIZE: **44.5 cm (17½ in) including tail of 19.5 cm (7¾ in)**

This large, formidable-looking lizard is adorned with spiny scales above its ears, at the back of its head and behind its mouth. On its body are a mixture of small and enlarged keeled scales. Adults have throat pouches or beards which are bordered with spiny scales. Most bearded dragons are semi-arboreal and feed on insects, flowers and soft plant growth in low vegetation.

The female bearded dragon lays 10 to 20 eggs in a nest which she digs in the soil. She covers the eggs with soil and, warmed by the sun, they incubate in the pit for about 3 months.

NAME: **Soa-soa Water Dragon,** *Hydrosaurus amboinensis*
RANGE: **New Guinea, Moluccas, Sulawesi**
HABITAT: **rain forest**
SIZE: **110 cm (43¼ in), including tail of 75 cm (29½ in)**

One of the largest agamids, the soa-soa is a powerfully built lizard with strong forefeet. The adult male has a showy crest on the base of the tail which can be erected, supported by bony extensions of the tail vertebrae. As its name suggests, this is an aquatic lizard, usually found close to rivers. It can swim well, propelling itself with its laterally compressed tail, and run on its hind legs on land.

Despite its formidable appearance, the soa-soa feeds largely on plants, particularly tender leaves; it also consumes insects and millipedes. It reproduces by laying eggs.

NAME: **Eastern Water Dragon,** *Physignathus leseueri*
RANGE: **E. Australia**
HABITAT: **coasts, forested slopes**
SIZE: **73 cm (28¾ in), including tail of 50 cm (19¾ in)**

The eastern water dragon varies in coloration over its wide range, but always has a long, powerful tail and a crest running along the length of its body and tail. A semi-aquatic, tree-living lizard, it lies on a branch overhanging a river or stream and, if disturbed, will tumble down into the water. It also forages on rocky seashores. Its diet is varied, including insects, small aquatic animals such as frogs, terrestrial animals and fruit and berries. The breeding female lays about 8 eggs under a rock or in a burrow she digs in the soil. The eggs hatch in 10 to 14 weeks.

THORNY DEVIL

FLYING DRAGON

FRILLED LIZARD

PRINCELY MASTIGURE

COMMON AGAMA

SOA-SOA WATER DRAGON (male)

BEARDED DRAGON

EASTERN WATER DRAGON

ARABIAN TOAD-HEADED AGAMID

Chameleons

NAME: **Jackson's Chameleon**, *Chamaeleo jacksonii*
RANGE: **E. Africa: Uganda, Tanzania to N. Mozambique**
HABITAT: **savanna vegetation**
SIZE: **11–12 cm (4¼–4¾ in)**

The three prominent horns on his head make the male Jackson's chameleon instantly recognizable. The female has only one small horn on the snout and rudimentary horns by each eye. Usually coloured a drab green, this chameleon resembles lichen on the bark of a tree.

One of the live-bearing species in the chameleon family, the female Jackson's chameleon may carry 20 to 40 eggs, but only 10 or so young ever actually survive. At birth, the young are about 5.5 cm (2¼ in) long and have two tiny horns in front of the eyes and a conical scale in the position of the middle horn.

NAME: **Meller's Chameleon**, *Chamaeleo melleri*
RANGE: **E. Africa: Tanzania, Malawi**
HABITAT: **savanna vegetation**
SIZE: **54–58 cm (21¼–22¾ in) including tail of 28–29 cm (11–11½ in)**

The largest chameleon found outside Madagascar, the male Meller's chameleon has only a tiny snout horn, which is also present in the female. Its body is distinctively marked with broad yellow stripes and black spots. As it sits on a branch, the chameleon often sways slightly, as a leaf might do in a breeze, and this, combined with its camouflaging coloration and patterning, makes it extremely hard to detect in foliage, despite its large size. Meller's chameleons feed on small birds, as well as on insects.

NAME: **Flap-necked Chameleon,** *Chamaeleo dilepis*
RANGE: **tropical and southern Africa**
HABITAT: **forest, scrubland**
SIZE: **25–36.5 cm (9¾–14¼ in)**

This aggressive chameleon has lobes of membranous skin at the back of its head which it erects in threat when it meets another member of its own species. It may raise only the lobe on the side of the opponent. A tree- and bush-dwelling species, it descends to the ground only to move from one tree to another or to lay eggs. Its coloration varies with the background; it is green when among leaves and yellow or reddish-brown when on bark. When angry or alarmed, for example when confronting the boomslang (tree snake), its main enemy, the chameleon turns dark blackish-green with yellow and white spots and makes hissing sounds.

The female lays 30 to 40 eggs in a hole she digs in the ground and then conceals the nest with grass and twigs. The eggs hatch in about 3 months.

CHAMAELEONIDAE:
Chameleon Family

The chameleons are probably the most specialized group of tree-living lizards, superbly adapted in both structural and behavioural ways. About 85 species are known; most live in Africa and Madagascar, but a few occur in Asia and there is one European species. Although primarily an arboreal group, a few species are ground-living.

Most chameleons are between 15 and 30 cm (6 and 11¾ in) in length, but a few are smaller, and one species in Madagascar reaches 70 to 80 cm (27½ to 31½ in). Whatever their size, all chameleons are recognizable by certain characteristic attributes. The typical chameleon has a body which is flattened from side to side; the head often has prominent crests or horns, and the large eyes are protuberant and can be moved independently of one another to locate insect prey. The toes on hind and forefeet are arranged to provide a pincerlike grip on branches: each foot divides clearly, with three toes on one side and two on the other. The muscular prehensile tail can be curled around a branch and helps the chameleon to stay immobile as it watches for prey.

Although several groups of lizards are able to change the colour of their skins, usually for camouflage purposes, the chameleon is the most accomplished. Camouflage helps the chameleon in its slow, stalking approach to prey animals and also helps to hide it from predators. The mechanism behind the chameleon's colour change abilities is complex. The pattern of pigmentation in the skin cells is controlled by the nervous system, and pigment can be spread out or contracted, thus lightening or darkening the skin. The strength of the light seems to be the most important influence on the mechanism.

Perhaps, however, the most extraordinary adaptive feature of the chameleons is their protrusible tongue. It can be shot out, from its tongue-bone support, to capture insects a body-length away from the reptile; at the tip of the tongue is a sticky pad to which the insect adheres. The chameleon has superb eyesight, which enables it to take accurate aim at the prey.

Chameleons generally reproduce by laying eggs, which the mother buries in a hole in the ground. A few African species, however, give birth to live young. In these forms, completely developed young chameleons grow inside their egg membranes, but free themselves from these enclosures immediately after the eggs are laid.

NAME: **European Chameleon**, *Chamaeleo chamaeleon*
RANGE: **S. Spain and Portugal, Crete, N. Africa, Canary Islands**
HABITAT: **bushes in dry country**
SIZE: **25–28 cm (9¾–11 in)**

The only chameleon to occur in Europe, this species is usually yellowish-brown with dark bands on the body, but may turn green when among grass or other green vegetation. When alarmed, it turns very dark and inflates its body with air so as to appear larger than its true size. In vegetated areas, this chameleon lives in bushes and descends to the ground only to lay eggs. In North Africa, however, in areas of sparse plant growth, it is a ground-dweller and lives in holes, which it digs itself, on the outskirts of oases. It feeds on insects, particularly locusts.

At mating time, males fight one another for females, and paired males and females may also fight. The female lays 20 to 30 eggs which she buries in the ground.

NAME: *Brooksia spectrum*
RANGE: **Cameroon, Gabon to E. Africa**
HABITAT: **forest floor**
SIZE: **7.5–9 cm (3–3½ in)**

This tiny, dusty-brown chameleon closely resembles the dead leaves among which it lives on the forest floor. The effect is enhanced by the stumpy tail, little peaks on the head and body and the irregular lines on the body which mimic leaf veins. There are two tiny appendages on the snout. Its legs are extremely thin and bony and the tail is not prehensile — as a ground-living chameleon it has no need of the fifth limb so useful to tree-dwelling species. It rarely changes colour; again, it has little need, being so well camouflaged already. Like all chameleons, it moves slowly and deliberately and may remain still for hours. It feeds on insects.

Little is known of the breeding habits, but females are believed to lay 3 to 6 eggs in a clutch.

NAME: *Rhampholeon marshalli*
RANGE: **Africa: Zimbabwe, Mozambique**
HABITAT: **forest on mountain slopes**
SIZE: **3.5–7.5 cm (1¼–3 in)**

The shape of this chameleon, with its flattened body and highly arched back, contributes to its leaflike appearance as it sits, swaying gently from side to side as if blowing in the wind. Rows of light-coloured tubercles scattered over the body are particularly prominent in males. Females are usually twice the size of males. Much of this chameleon's life is spent among the leaf litter of the forest floor.

The female lays 12 to 18 eggs.

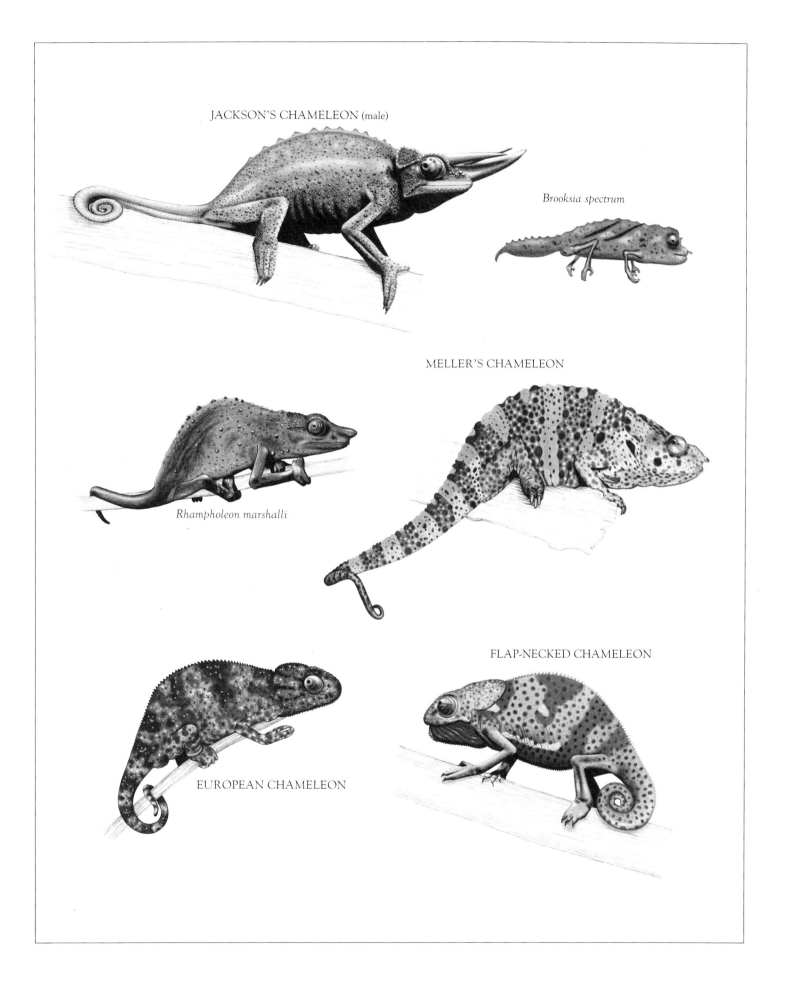

JACKSON'S CHAMELEON (male)

Brooksia spectrum

MELLER'S CHAMELEON

Rhampholeon marshalli

FLAP-NECKED CHAMELEON

EUROPEAN CHAMELEON

Geckos I

NAME: **Tokay Gecko,** *Gekko gekko*
RANGE: **Asia, Indonesia**
HABITAT: **in or near houses**
SIZE: **28 cm (11 in)**

One of the largest and most common geckos, the tokay gecko is believed to bring good luck to the houses whose walls it frequents. It feeds on insects, particularly cockroaches, and on young lizards, mice and small birds, all of which it seizes in its powerful jaws. The male makes his loud barking call, "tokeh" or "gek-oh", most frequently in the mating season; the female is mute.

The female tokay gecko lays 2 sticky-surfaced eggs, which are usually stuck fast to a perpendicular object and are almost impossible to remove without breaking. The same locations are used year after year, and it is common to find 8 to 10 sets of eggs together, all laid by different females and in various stages of incubation.

NAME: **White-spotted Gecko,** *Tarentola*
annularis
RANGE: **Africa: Libya, Egypt, Sudan,**
Ethiopia, Somalia
HABITAT: **trees, rocks, ruins in semi-**
desert
SIZE: **20.5 cm (8 in)**

The body colour of these geckos varies according to the surface they are on: geckos on the black rocks above the first Nile Cateract are black, while those found on white-washed walls are almost white.

Aggressive, active creatures, they feed primarily on insects but also eat spiders and lizards. They are able to survive long periods without water, although they drink eagerly when the opportunity presents itself.

Mating is triggered by the arrival of the rains, and the female gecko lays her eggs in a crevice or hole in a rock or wall.

NAME: **Leopard Gecko,** *Eublepharius*
macularius
RANGE: **Afganistan, S. Turkistan,**
Pakistan, W. India
HABITAT: **dry, rocky regions**
SIZE: **up to 30 cm (11¾ in)**

Also known as the panther gecko, this chunky lizard has a spotted body and a large head. Unlike most geckos, which have fused transparent eyelids, this species is one of the few with movable eyelids — a primitive characteristic in the gecko family. Its legs are long and thin and it holds its body well off the ground when it runs. Leopard geckos feed on grasshoppers, scorpions, beetles and spiders. They are nocturnal and hide during the day under rocks or in burrows in the sand.

During the year, the female lays several clutches, each of 2 eggs.

GEKKONIDAE: Gecko Family

Throughout the tropical, subtropical and warm temperate zones of the world are distributed some 675 species of gecko. These lizards may inhabit forests, swamps, deserts or mountainous areas; in fact, any place with sufficient insect life for them to feed on and where nights do not become too cold. They range in size from 5 to 30 cm (2 to 11¾ in), although most are between 7 and 15 cm (2¾ and 6 in) long.

The typical gecko has a flattened head and a body with soft skin, containing many minute scales. Most are nocturnal animals and have enormous eyes, each with a permanently closed transparent eyelid. Many have "friction pads" of specialized scales under the toes which enable them to climb easily up vertical surfaces and even to walk upside-down, on a ceiling for instance.

The males of many of the nocturnal species are among the most vocal lizards and make loud, repetitive calls. Females lay only 1 to 3 eggs at a time but may breed several times a year; the young are already almost half the length of their parents when they hatch. The eggs of most geckos are harder-shelled than those of other lizards; they are quite soft when laid and harden after a period of exposure to air.

NAME: **Web-footed Gecko,**
Palmatogecko rangei
RANGE: **S.W. Africa: Namib desert**
HABITAT: **sand-dunes, rocks**
SIZE: **12.5 cm (5 in)**

This extremely rare species, which lives on the seaward slopes of the Namib desert where rain is almost unknown, absorbs moisture from the sea breezes and from the mists that roll in from the sea. It also laps dew from the stones and licks its own eyes for moisture.

Since this gecko lives on the ground, it has no need of friction pads on its feet for climbing vertical surfaces; instead, its almost clawless toes are connected by webs which act like snowshoes in the soft sand. When running, the gecko holds its body well off the hot ground, and its feet leave little or no trace of its movements. The webbed feet are also used for burrowing into the sand to escape from predators or from the blistering sun. The gecko makes a chamber in which it lies with its head facing the entrance, waiting to pounce on the termites, beetles, flies and worms that are its main food. If a predator should try to pull it out, the gecko clings to the side of the chamber with its strong tail, engaging in a tug-of-war.

NAME: **Kuhl's Gecko,** *Ptychozoon kuhli*
RANGE: **S.E. Asia, Indonesia, Borneo**
HABITAT: **forest**
SIZE: **15 cm (6 in)**

The geckos of this genus, often known as the fringed or even "flying" geckos, have fringes of skin along the sides of the head, limbs, body and tail, and webs between the toes. When jumping or falling from trees, the gecko extends its legs and tail to expand the flaps and uses them like a parachute. Perhaps even more important is the camouflage the fringes give as the gecko rests on the branch of a tree: it presses the skin flaps down against the bark, thus removing any shadows and breaking up its outline.

The female Kuhl's gecko lays her eggs in November. The eggs, coated with a sticky substance when laid, adhere to each other and to the branch of the tree and gradually develop a hard shell. The young geckos hatch the following May.

NAME: **Marbled Gecko,** *Phyllodactylus*
porphyreus
RANGE: **South Africa, Australia**
HABITAT: **arid mountain slopes**
SIZE: **11.5 cm (4½ in)**

This active little gecko lives in cracks in rocks or beneath stones and varies in coloration according to its surroundings. It feeds on insects and is often parasitized by mites.

The female marbled gecko lays her eggs under a stone or on a tree, where they remain until they hatch out approximately 115 days later. The newly hatched young are about 2 cm (¾ in) long, with tails that are over half their body length.

NAME: **Brook's Gecko,** *Hemidactylus*
brookii
RANGE: **Asia, Africa, South America,**
East and West Indies
HABITAT: **coastal plains to upland**
savanna to 2,100 m (7,000 ft)
SIZE: **15 cm (6 in)**

This unusually widespread gecko lives under stones, in cracks in rocks, in abandoned termite mounds, beneath fallen tree trunks and even under heaps of garden debris.

With its sharply curving claws, it climbs with great agility up even vertical surfaces. It feeds on insects and at night will enter houses to prey on those which are attracted to the light. It is difficult to ascertain the exact length of this species since adults rarely have their long tails intact; although the tail breaks off easily, muscles in the main tail artery contract speedily to prevent any undue loss of blood.

In the breeding season the female Brook's gecko lays 2 eggs.

BROOK'S GECKO

WHITE-SPOTTED GECKO

MARBLED GECKO

WEB-FOOTED GECKO

TOKAY GECKO

LEOPARD GECKO

KUHL'S GECKO

Geckos 2, Scaly-foot Lizards

NAME: **Leaf-tailed Gecko,** *Uroplatus fimbriatus*
RANGE: **Madagascar**
HABITAT: **forest**
SIZE: **20.5 cm (8 in)**

A flat-bodied gecko with large bulging eyes, the leaf-tailed gecko's mottled body blends excellently with bark or lichen. It lies with its body pressed against a branch or trunk of a tree and the small scales bordering its legs and sides reduce any shadow. In addition to this camouflage, it can change the intensity of its coloration, becoming darker by night and lighter again in the morning. When alarmed, it turns dark-brown or black. The broad, flat tail can be rolled up dorsally — toward the back — and is used as a fifth limb for holding on to branches.

Mainly active at night, this gecko feeds on insects. Each individual has a preferred resting place where, after a meal, it retires to clean itself, using its tongue to lick over its whole body, even the eyes.

NAME: **Green Day Gecko,** *Heteropholis manukanus*
RANGE: **N. New Zealand (Marlborough Sound, Stephen's Island)**
HABITAT: **forest, scrub**
SIZE: **12.5–16.5 cm (5–6½ in)**

Unlike most geckos, the green day gecko is active in the daytime when it forages in trees for insects and small invertebrates. It is found mainly on the manuka, or tea-tree, (*Leptospermum scoparium*). Its bright green coloration has yellow undertones, and the female's belly is yellowish-green, the male's bluish-green. In both sexes the soles of the feet are yellowish. The head is rather large and the snout deep and blunt.

Most geckos lay eggs, but the female of this species gives birth to 2, occasionally only 1, live young. The young are similar in appearance to the adults.

Numbers of these geckos have fallen because large areas of their forest and scrub habitat have been cleared for development.

NAME: *Phelsuma vinsoni*
RANGE: **Mauritius and neighbouring islands**
HABITAT: **forest**
SIZE: **17.5 cm (6¾ in)**

An unusual gecko species with its vivid coloration, the male *Phelsuma vinsoni* has bright red spots on a blue and green back and brown lines on the head and neck region. The female has similar patterning but is less vivid and is tinged with brown or grey. This gecko is also unusual in that it is active during the day; most are nocturnal. A good climber, it is often found on screwpine trees, the fruit of which attracts the insects on which it feeds. Fruit such as bananas and the nectar of flowers sometimes supplement the gecko's diet.

The female gecko lays 2 sticky-surfaced eggs which are usually left attached to a branch; several females may lay their eggs together. They hatch after 9 to 12 weeks, depending on the temperature, and the young geckos measure about 12 cm (4¾ in), most of which is tail.

PYGOPODIDAE:
Scaly-foot Lizard Family

The scaly-foots, or snake lizards, are one of the groups of lizards which, although they are limbless and snakelike, are anatomically different from true snakes. There are about 14 known species, all found in Australia or New Guinea.

Although externally so similar to snakes, the scaly-foots are, in fact, most closely related to geckos and share certain characteristics with them, such as fused eyelids and their ability to make sounds. Their hind limbs are present as vestigial scaly flaps, and the tail is extremely long. The flat, fleshy tongue is slightly forked and can be extended well out of the mouth.

NAME: **Burton's Snake-lizard,** *Lialis burtonis*
RANGE: **Australia: central areas, Queensland; New Guinea**
HABITAT: **semi-desert, rain forest**
SIZE: **up to 61 cm (24 in)**

The most widespread species of its family, this snake-lizard is able to adapt to the contrasting habitats of rain forest and semi-desert. A ground-dweller, it hides in clumps of grass or under plant debris. Its colour and pattern vary but they are not related to geographical distribution, and it always has a distinctive brown stripe on each side of the head. The snout is long and pointed.

Active during both day and night, Burton's snake-lizard feeds on insects, skinks and other small lizards. Its long, pointed, backward-curving teeth enable it to overcome quite large prey, which it seizes with a quick snap of its jaws and swallows whole.

Unlike other snake-lizards, which make geckolike barks or soft squeaks, this lizard emits a long drawn-out note. The female lays 2 or 3 large elongate eggs which have parchmentlike shells.

NAME: **Hooded Scaly-foot,** *Pygopus nigriceps*
RANGE: **Western Australia**
HABITAT: **dry inland country, coastal forest**
SIZE: **46 cm (18 in)**

Also known as the black-headed or western scaly-foot, this species has a tail that is slightly longer than its body and a rounded snout. The hind limbs are present as scaly flaps, each containing miniature leg bones and four toes. These flaps usually lie flat against the body, but when the animal is handled or injured, they are held out at right angles.

If threatened, the hooded scaly-foot mimics the poisonous elapid snake, *Denisonia gouldii*, to try to deter its enemy: it draws back its head, bends its neck into an S-shape, puffs out its throat slightly and hisses. It feeds on insects and small lizards and is most active at dusk and at night. The female lays 2 eggs.

NAME: *Delma nasuta*
RANGE: **Australia: Western and Northern Territories, South Australia**
HABITAT: **sandy and stony desert, arid scrub**
SIZE: **30 cm (11¾ in) including tail of 22 cm (8½ in)**

The 3 species of scaly-foot in the genus *Delma* are all slender bodied and move exactly like snakes, resembling the smaller elapid snakes of Australia. They feed on insects and small lizards both at night and during the day, but species living in the hot desert areas of central Australia are strictly nocturnal. The hind limbs are present as tiny but movable flaps which are held against the body. The female lays 2 eggs.

NAME: *Aprasia striolata*
RANGE: **Australia: isolated populations in S. W. Western Australia, S. Australia to W. Victoria; Northern Territory**
HABITAT: **varied, sandy or loamy soils**
SIZE: **15 cm (6 in)**

There are 4 species in the genus *Aprasia*, all of which are alike in habits and appearance. A small burrowing creature, this species has a rounded snout and inconspicuous flaps which are vestiges of its hind limbs. Its tail is short. It feeds on insects and lizards and is mainly active in the daytime. The females of this genus of lizards generally lay 2 eggs at a time.

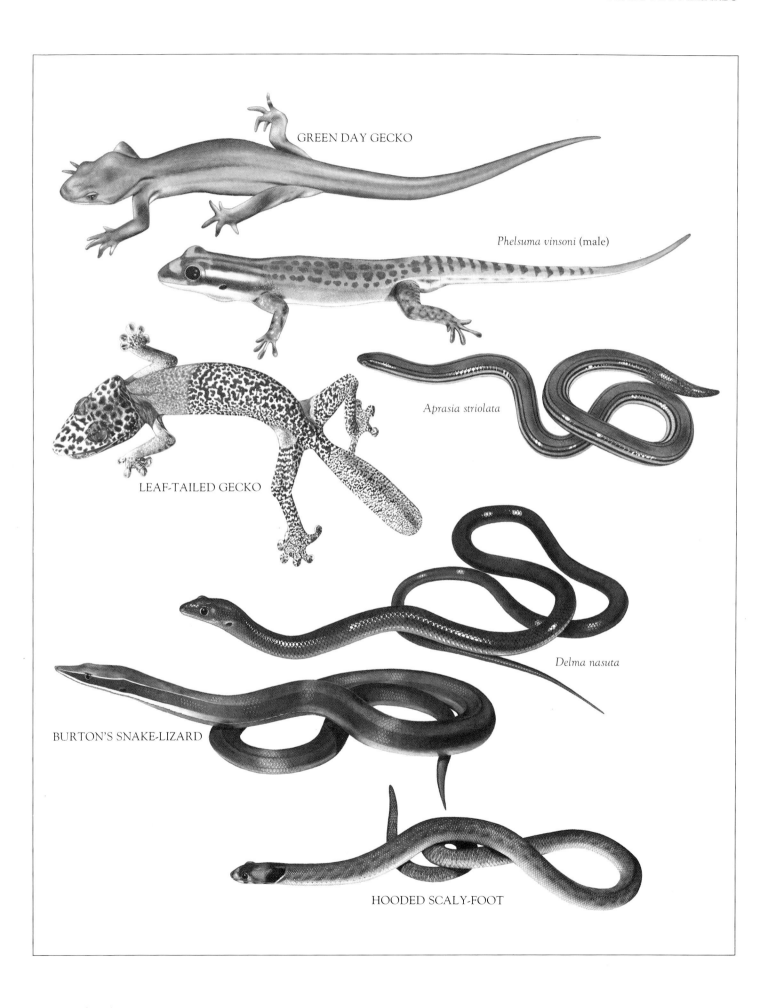

GREEN DAY GECKO

Phelsuma vinsoni (male)

LEAF-TAILED GECKO

Aprasia striolata

Delma nasuta

BURTON'S SNAKE-LIZARD

HOODED SCALY-FOOT

Night Lizards, Teiid Lizards

XANTUSIIDAE: Night Lizard Family

As their name suggests, night lizards are nocturnal, beginning their hunting activities at dusk and spending the daylight hours hidden among rocks and under stones. There are about 18 species in the family, found in the southwest of the USA, Central America and Cuba, mostly in rocky, arid habitats. They feed on nocturnal insects.

Night lizards have a superficial resemblance to geckos, with their immobile eyelids, the lower of which have transparent "windows". Unlike the geckos, they have scales on the back and belly and shields on the head. All night lizards give birth to live young which develop inside the mother's body, nourished by a form of placenta.

NAME: **Desert Night Lizard, *Xantusia vigilis***
RANGE: **S. W. USA: Nevada, Utah to California; Mexico**
HABITAT: **rocky, arid and semi–arid land**
SIZE: **9.5–12.5 cm (3¾–5 in)**

The desert night lizard varies in coloration over its range but is marked with many small dark spots. It frequents yucca plants and agaves and feeds on termites, ants, beetles and flies, which it finds among vegetation or rocks.

Night lizards give birth to live young. They mate in early summer, usually May or June, and 1 to 3 young are born, tail first, a few months later.

TEIIDAE: Teiid Lizard Family

There are about 230 species in this exclusively American family, the majority of which live in South America. Teiids are slender lizards with thin, whiplike tails and characteristic long, deeply divided tongues, which they use to search for food. Most species have scales on the back and belly.

In many ways, teiids represent the New World equivalent of the lacertid lizards. Most species are ground-living, feeding on a variety of small animals, but some have become specialized for a particular way of life, for example the caiman lizard, which is semi-aquatic and feeds on snails.

Teiids reproduce by laying eggs. Most must mate first in the normal way, but in a few unisexual species no mating is necessary. In these teiids, all individuals are female and can lay eggs, which do not need to be fertilized and which hatch into more females, so completely dispensing with the need for males.

NAME: **Caiman Lizard, *Dracaena guianensis***
RANGE: **N. E. South America**
HABITAT: **swampy flooded ground, often woodland bordering rivers**
SIZE: **1.2 m (4 ft)**

The large, powerful caiman lizard has an oarlike, laterally flattened tail and rough, horny, platelike scales along its back. It inhabits areas which are flooded for much of the time, except when the rivers are at their lowest, and frequents the resulting pools and ponds. It spends much of the day in water and dives and swims well, using its tail for propulsion. At night, it finds shelter above water level, often in trees or bushes. It feeds almost entirely on aquatic snails, taking the snail in its jaws, then raising its head so that the snail slides back into its mouth, where it is broken up by the huge, crushing back teeth. The pieces of shell are spat out and the soft body swallowed.

The female caiman lizard, having mated, lays eggs which she buries, often in a deserted arboreal termites' nest.

NAME: **Common Tegu, *Tupinambis teguixin***
RANGE: **Central America, N. South America**
HABITAT: **forest, woodland**
SIZE: **1.2–1.4 m (4–4½ ft), including tail of 70–85 cm (27½–33½ in)**

A robust lizard with a long cylindrical tail, the tegu has prominent yellow markings on its dark body. It frequents dense undergrowth and is also found in cultivated areas where food is abundant. Chickens and their eggs are included in its diet, as well as small mammals, frogs, large insects, worms and some fruit and leaves. It hunts by day and hides in a burrow at night and in cool weather. A formidable opponent, the tegu will lash out at an enemy with its powerful tail before attacking with its jaws. However, it will run away from danger when possible, and juveniles are able to run on their hind legs. Local tribespeople catch the tegu and use the yellow body fat as a cure for inflammations.

The female tegu lays her eggs in an inhabited arboreal termites' nest, tearing the outer wall open to deposit her 6 to 8 eggs inside. The ever-vigilant termites then come along and repair the wall of their nest, thus sealing the tegu eggs safely away from predators and changes in temperature or humidity while they develop. The newly hatched young must break out of the termites' nest by themselves.

NAME: **Jungle Runner, *Ameiva ameiva***
RANGE: **Central America, South America, east of the Andes; introduced in USA: Florida**
HABITAT: **open grassland**
SIZE: **15–20 cm (6–7¾ in)**

A ground-living, extremely active lizard, the jungle runner emerges in the morning to forage for food, flicking out its long forked tongue to search for insects, spiders, snails and other small invertebrates and small lizards. The protrusible tongue is tactile and can also detect scents. In coastal regions, the jungle runner may be found in burrows, such as those made by crabs and, in Panama, it is reported to be extending its normal range by moving into areas recently cleared by man.

The male jungle runner is usually larger than the female and is marked with conspicuous light spots, whereas the female has distinctive stripes along her body. After mating, the female lays a clutch of 1 to 4 eggs.

NAME: **Teyu, *Teius teyou***
RANGE: **S. E. Brazil to Argentina**
HABITAT: **open, rocky land**
SIZE: **30 cm (11¾ in)**

One of the most numerous and widespread of South American teiids, the adaptable teyu lives wherever there is open land with some rock cover. For shelter, it makes a tunnel under a large stone that leads down to a small chamber, measuring about 2.5 cm by 4 cm (1 in by 1½ in). Here it lies, curled in a U-shape, its body in the chamber and its head and long tail in the tunnel. It feeds on insects and, occasionally, on spiders.

NAME: **Strand Racerunner, *Cnemidophorus lemniscatus***
RANGE: **Central America to N. South America; Trinidad, Tobago**
HABITAT: **lowland plains, open regions of flood–plain forest**
SIZE: **30 cm (11¾ in)**

One of the fastest-moving of all the lizards, the strand racerunner is always on the move, continually darting off in different directions and sometimes running on its hind legs. Speeds of 24 to 28 km/h (15 to 17 mph) have been recorded over short distances. It is active during the day and, although mainly ground-dwelling, it also climbs low trees and bushes in search of food. A long-bodied lizard, it has an elongate, tapering, ridged tail; its snout may be blunt or pointed.

To mate, the male sits astride the female, holding the skin of her neck in his mouth. He curves his body around hers while copulating. The female lays 4 to 6 eggs which hatch some 8 to 10 weeks later.

CAIMAN LIZARD

DESERT NIGHT LIZARD

STRAND RACERUNNER

COMMON TEGU

JUNGLE RUNNER

TEYU

Skinks I

NAME: **Legless Skink,** *Acontias* **sp.**
RANGE: South Africa, Madagascar
HABITAT: sandy regions
SIZE: 10 cm (4 in)

Legless skinks spend most of their lives in their underground burrows. They are indeed limbless, with long cylindrical bodies and short tails. Their eyes and ears are protected by scales, and their lower eyelids are equipped with transparent "windows", to enable them to see when burrowing without getting soil in their eyes. Their bodies are covered with hard, smooth scales, enabling them to move easily through the earth. They also move quickly on the surface, using snakelike undulations of the body. Legless skinks are largely insectivorous but may also eat small invertebrates and frogs.

Females bear live young, producing litters of 3 or 4 at a time.

NAME: **Round-bodied Skink,** *Chalcides bedriagai*
RANGE: Spain, Portugal
HABITAT: varied, arid, sandy land, hilly areas, grassland
SIZE: up to 16 cm (6¼ in)

An elongate, short-legged species, this skink keeps out of sight in ground vegetation or burrows into loose sand. It is usually a buff or greyish-brown with dark-edged markings, and its scales are large, smooth and shiny. It varies somewhat in colour and proportions over its range: southern individuals, for example, have shorter legs than the western populations, while those in the east have medium-length legs. Round-bodied skinks feed on a variety of small invertebrates.

Females give birth to 2 or 3 fully formed live young, which have developed inside the body, nourished by a form of placenta.

NAME: **Sundeval's Skink,** *Riopa sundevalli*
RANGE: Africa: Zambia to South Africa
HABITAT: open plains, sandy savanna
SIZE: up to 18 cm (7 in)

A burrowing species, Sundeval's skink has tiny limbs and smooth scales. It comes to the surface in search of food — insects and their larvae, spiders, woodlice and soft snails — and may hide under stones or leaf debris. Termite hills and manure heaps are also favourite spots for these skinks. On the ground, the skink moves in a snakelike fashion, its tiny limbs of little use. The tail breaks away easily, and adults are seldom seen with a complete tail.

Females lay 2 to 6 eggs, usually 4, in a nest underground or in a termite mound. The newly hatched young skinks measure 5 cm (2 in).

SCINCIDAE: Skink Family

One of the largest lizard families, with many hundreds of species, skinks occur on every continent except Antarctica. They are most abundant in Southeast Asia and the Australasian region.

Skinks live on or below the ground and are normally smooth-scaled, with elongate, rounded bodies and tapering tails. Their legs are short, and some burrowing skinks have tiny legs or none at all. Many families of lizards include species with reduced or no limbs, but this is particularly common in the skink family. The majority are between 8 and 35 cm (3¼ and 13¾ in) in length, although there are a few giant forms.

Most skinks feed on insects and small invertebrates; the giant forms, however, are herbivorous. Their reproductive habits vary: most species lay eggs but some give birth to live young.

NAME: **Sandfish,** *Scincus philbyi*
RANGE: Saudi Arabia
HABITAT: sandy desert
SIZE: up to 21 cm (8¼ in)

Unlike most burrowing skinks, this species retains well-developed legs and feet. Its digits are flattened and have fringes of scales to help it move easily over loose sand. The body of the sandfish is robust and cylindrical, and it has a broad, wedge-shaped snout. The sandfish is active through the heat of the day, for it spends most of its time under the surface of the sand, looking for prey such as beetles and millipedes. It pushes its way along, literally seeming to swim through the sand, hence its name.

The female sandfish gives birth to fully formed live young which have developed inside her body.

NAME: *Feylinia cussori*
RANGE: tropical Africa
HABITAT: forest
SIZE: 35 cm (13¾ in)

A large burrowing skink, *Feylinia cussori* has a rather flattened head, which merges smoothly with its limbless cylindrical body. There are no external eardrums and its tiny eyes are protected by transparent scales. It is often found under decaying wood and feeds largely on termites, which it locates by the sounds they make in the wood.

The female bears litters of 2 or 3 live young which have developed inside her body. There is a local superstition that *Feylinia* can enter the human body whenever it desires and, when it leaves again, the person dies.

NAME: **Great Plains Skink,** *Eumeces obsoletus*
RANGE: S. central USA: Wyoming and Nebraska to Arizona and Texas; Mexico
HABITAT: rocky grassland, usually near water
SIZE: 16.5–35 cm (6½–13¾ in)

The largest North American skink, the Great Plains skink has well-developed, sturdy limbs, and its body is spotted with dark brown or black; these spots may merge in places to give the impression of lengthwise stripes. Active in the daytime, it feeds on insects, spiders and small lizards. It is an aggressive skink and will bite readily if alarmed.

The Great Plains skink is unusual among lizards for the degree of maternal care it displays. A few weeks after mating in April or May, the female lays 17 to 21 eggs in a nest which she makes beneath a rock. She guards the eggs while they incubate and turns them regularly to ensure even warming. When, a couple of months later, the eggs begin to hatch, the female rubs them and presses them with her body, stimulating the young to move and then to wriggle free of the shell. For a further 10 days after hatching, she attends her young, cleaning each one regularly. Juvenile Great Plains skinks are generally black with blue tails and some white spots. This coloration gradually fades as the skinks mature.

NAME: **Florida Sand Skink,** *Neoseps reynoldsi*
RANGE: USA: central Florida
HABITAT: sandhills
SIZE: 10–13 cm (4–5 in)

This small skink is an expert digger and burrower: using its chisel-shaped snout, it burrows speedily into the sand, undulating its body as it goes, as if swimming. Its limbs are tiny and it has only one digit on each forelimb and two on each hind limb. It feeds on termites and beetle larvae, which it locates by the sound vibrations they cause. Although it is active in the daytime and comes to the surface to shelter under logs and other debris, the sand skink is a secretive species and rarely seen. If alarmed, it quickly buries itself.

Sand skinks mate in spring and the female lays 2 eggs.

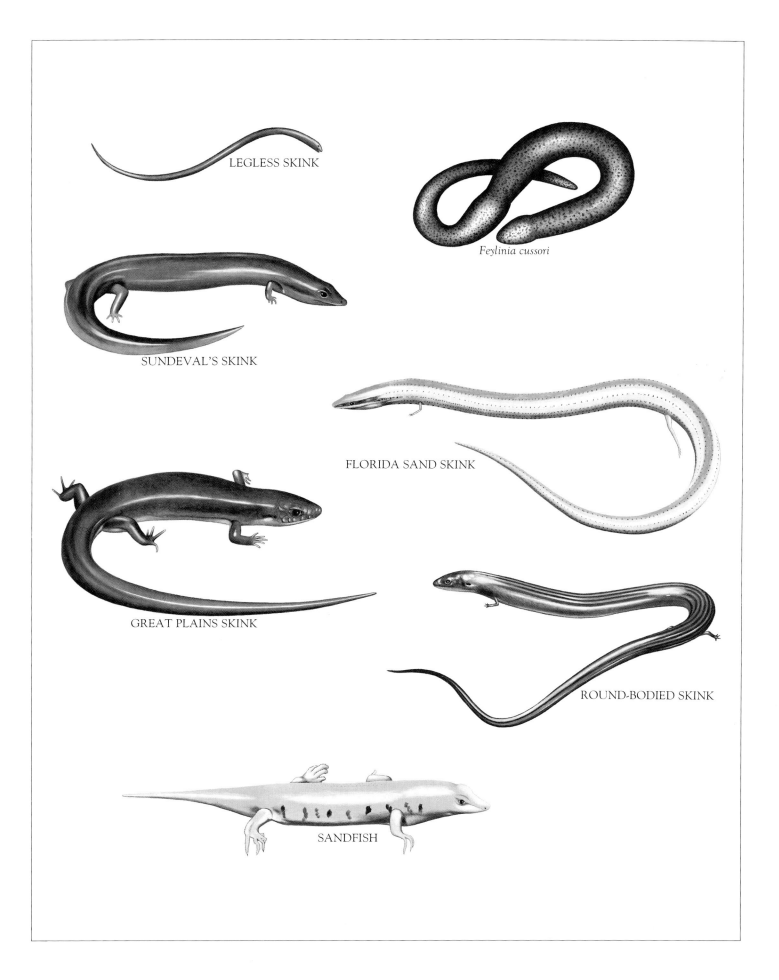

LEGLESS SKINK

Feylinia cussori

SUNDEVAL'S SKINK

FLORIDA SAND SKINK

GREAT PLAINS SKINK

ROUND-BODIED SKINK

SANDFISH

Skinks 2

NAME: Mabuya, *Mabuya wrightii*
RANGE: Seychelles
HABITAT: granite islands with guano deposits
SIZE: 31 cm (12¼ in) including tail of up to 18 cm (7 in)

The stocky-bodied mabuya has well-developed hind limbs with long digits. Its snout is slightly elongate and blunt. A fast-moving, ground-dwelling lizard, the mabuya is active in the daytime and has a great need of warmth. Mabuyas are usually found on the smaller islands of the Seychelles, often in close association with the nesting colonies of seabirds. In the breeding season, mabuyas feed on birds' eggs, especially those of terns, which they break by rolling them off rocks or branches. They then lap up the contents. Their diet is not known outside the birds' breeding season.

Most mabuya species give birth to live young, but the exact details of the breeding habits of this particular mabuya have not been observed. One South African mabuya species, M. *trivittata*, is one of the few reptiles to assist her newborn young. She helps the young to escape from the soft membranes in which they are born, by tearing the coverings open with her teeth.

NAME: Spiny-tailed Skink, *Egernia stokesii*
RANGE: Western Australia through arid interior to Queensland, New South Wales and South Australia
HABITAT: stony hills, mountains
SIZE: up to 27 cm (10½ in)

The spiny-tailed skink is a most unusual species, with a stout body covered with rough-edged, sometimes spiny scales. The tail is short and much flattened and particularly well endowed with spinous scales. All four limbs are strong and well developed. This skink frequents rocky areas, where it can shelter in deep crevices or under boulders; the spines on its tail make it virtually impossible to dislodge once it has wedged itself in such a hiding place. It is active during the day, when it basks in the sun and forages for insects within easy reach of its refuge. A gregarious species, it lives in colonies and the presence of spiny-tailed skinks in an area is signalled by their regular defecation sites, where small piles of faeces accumulate.

Spiny-tailed skinks are live-bearers. The female gives birth to about 5 fully formed young, which develop inside her body, nourished by a form of placenta. The young measure about 6 cm (2¼ in) at birth.

NAME: *Emoia cyanogaster*
RANGE: Australia: extreme N. Queensland; Indonesia
HABITAT: forest, banana groves
SIZE: up to 27 cm (10½ in)

A slender, glossy skink with a slim tapering tail, *Emoia cyanogaster* has a pointed, somewhat flattened snout. Its limbs, particularly the hind limbs, are long and well formed, with elongate digits. It is an agile, primarily tree-dwelling species and can jump easily from branch to branch. Much of its day is spent basking on low vegetation or sheltering among the trailing leaves of banana trees, but it often descends to the ground to search for food.

These skinks breed throughout the year, although with some seasonal fluctuations. The female usually lays 2 eggs at a time.

NAME: *Leiolopisma infrapunctatum*
RANGE: New Zealand
HABITAT: open country with some vegetation
SIZE: 24 cm (9½ in)

This smooth-scaled skink has beautiful markings, which may vary slightly in coloration and intensity but are usually constant in pattern. The most striking are the broad, broken bands of reddish-brown, which run from behind each eye, above the limbs, to the tail. The belly is usually yellow with scattered dark markings. The head and body are elongate and there is no distinct neck.

Active in the daytime, this skink often lives near petrel nesting sites. It basks in the sun but is easily scared and swiftly takes refuge at the least sign of disturbance. It feeds on small land-living invertebrates and insects. Mating takes place in spring, and the female gives birth to a litter of live young about 4 months later.

NAME: Western Blue-tongued Skink, *Tiliqua occipitalis*
RANGE: S. Australia
HABITAT: arid areas
SIZE: 45 cm (17¾ in)

The heavily built western blue-tongued skink has a stout body and large head but relatively small limbs. Bands of dark brown scales pattern its body and tail, and there are characteristic dark streaks behind each eye. It is active in the daytime and forages around on the ground for insects, snails and berries. A rabbit warren may be used for shelter.

The female gives birth to about 5 live young, each of which is distinctly banded with dark brown and yellow.

NAME: Prickly Forest Skink, *Tropidophorus queenslandiae*
RANGE: Australia: N. Queensland
HABITAT: rain forest
SIZE: 13–20 cm (5–7¾ in)

The prickly forest skink is easily distinguished from other Australian skinks by its covering of strongly keeled small scales. Its rounded tail is also covered with keeled scales, and its limbs are well developed. A nocturnal skink, it lives beneath plant debris or rotting logs on the forest floor, where its dark body with irregular pale markings keeps it well camouflaged. It is a slow-moving, sluggish skink which does not like to bask in sunlight and is usually found in a rather torpid state. Worms and soft-bodied insects are its main foods.

Little is known of the breeding biology of this skink, but several of the 20 *Tropidophorus* species are known to produce litters of 6 to 9 live young. These develop inside the mother's body and break from their thin shells as the eggs are laid.

NAME: Brown Skink, *Scincella lateralis* (previously *Lygosoma lateralis*)
RANGE: USA: New Jersey to Florida, west to Nebraska and Texas
HABITAT: humid forest, wooded grassland
SIZE: 8–13 cm (3¼–5 in)

This smooth, shiny skink, also known as the ground skink, has dark stripes on the sides of its body and a pale, often yellowish or whitish belly. Its body is long and slender and its legs well developed, with elongate digits on the hind feet. Like many skinks, the brown skink has movable eyelids with a transparent window in each lower lid; this feature enables it to see clearly even when it must close its eyes to avoid dirt getting into them when it is burrowing into cover. It lives on the ground and prefers areas with plenty of leaf litter in which to take shelter. Active in the daytime, particularly in warm, humid weather, it feeds mainly on insects and spiders. The closest relatives of this species live in Central America and Australia.

A prolific breeder, the female brown skink lays a clutch of 1 to 7 eggs every 4 or 5 weeks, with a maximum of about 5 clutches during the breeding season, which extends from April to August in most areas. Embryonic development is already well advanced when the eggs are laid, and the female does not tend the eggs further.

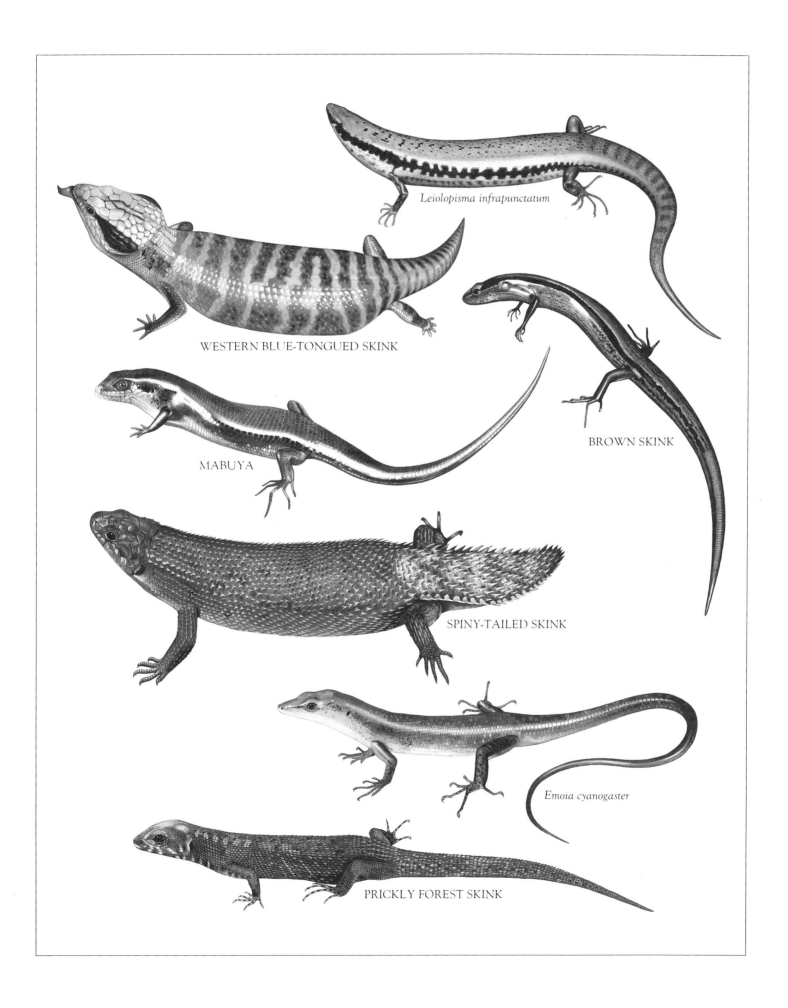

Leiolopisma infrapunctatum

WESTERN BLUE-TONGUED SKINK

BROWN SKINK

MABUYA

SPINY-TAILED SKINK

Emoia cyanogaster

PRICKLY FOREST SKINK

Lacertid Lizards

NAME: Green Lizard, *Lacerta viridis*
RANGE: Europe: Channel Islands, south to N. Spain, Sicily, Greece; east to S. W. Russia
HABITAT: open woodland, field edges, river banks, roadsides
SIZE: 30–45 cm (11¾–17¾ in) including tail of 20–30 cm (7¾–11¾ in)

Also known as the emerald lizard, this is the largest lizard found north of the Alps. Males are brilliant green, finely stippled with black, while females are more variable, often duller green or brownish. The coloration of mature adults is most vivid in the spring and fades as the year proceeds.

An adaptable lizard, the green lizard lives almost anywhere that there is dense vegetation but avoids arid areas. It is an agile climber and can move speedily up trees, bushes and walls to find a spot in which to bask in the sun. Insects and their larvae and small invertebrates, particularly spiders, are its main foods.

Solitary creatures for most of the year, green lizards mate in the spring, when males compete fiercely for females. When copulating, the male grasps the female with his jaws. She lays 4 to 21 eggs in a hole she digs in the soil. She covers the eggs with earth and they incubate for several months. In winter, green lizards hibernate in tree hollows or other crevices.

NAME: Viviparous Lizard, *Lacerta vivipara*
RANGE: Europe: Arctic Scandinavia, Britain, south to N. Spain, N. Italy, Yugoslavia; N. Asia
HABITAT: meadows, open woodland, marshes, any grassland
SIZE: 14–18 cm (5½–7 in)

The viviparous lizard is the only lizard found within the Arctic Circle. Its coloration is variable over its wide range, but this lizard is commonly grey or yellowish-brown, with pale spots and dark stripes on the back. In the hotter parts of its range, it is rarely found below 500 m (1,650 ft) except in humid areas, but it likes to bask in the sun for much of the day. Alert and agile, it is a fairly good climber and an excellent swimmer. Insects, spiders, earthworms, slugs and other small invertebrates are all part of its diet. It lives alone except in the hibernation and breeding seasons.

The breeding habits of this lizard are unique in its family, hence its name meaning "live-bearing". The 5 to 8 young develop inside the mother, feeding on the yolks of their eggs, and break out of their thin membranous shells fully formed, as they are expelled from her body or shortly afterwards.

LACERTIDAE:
Lacertid Lizard Family

About 180 species of lacertid lizard are distributed throughout Europe, Asia and Africa, excluding Madagascar. Within this range, they occur from the hottest tropical habitats to locations within the Arctic Circle. Most are ground-dwelling, but others live in trees or among rocks.

The elongate, long-tailed lacertids are mostly small to medium-sized lizards between 10 and 75 cm (4 and 29½ in) in total length. All have large scales on head and belly. Externally, males can generally be distinguished from females by their larger heads and shorter bodies. Almost all species reproduce by laying eggs, depositing their clutches in earth or sand.

Lacertids are highly territorial in their behaviour. Males in particular adopt characteristic threat postures to warn off intruders, with the head tilted upward and the throat expanded.

In common with many other lizard families, lacertids feed on small, mainly invertebrate prey animals. A few species, particularly island-dwelling forms, also consume large amounts of plant material.

NAME: Wall Lizard, *Lacerta muralis*
RANGE: Europe: N. France to N. Spain, S. Italy, Greece, east to Romania
HABITAT: dry, sunny areas; walls, rocks, tree trunks
SIZE: up to 23 cm (9 in)

A slender, flat-bodied reptile, the wall lizard has a tapering tail which may be up to twice its body length. The coloration and markings of this species are exceedingly variable over its range, but many individuals are brownish-red or grey, with dark markings. A sun-loving lizard, it spends much of the day basking on any form of wall, even near human habitation; in the midday heat, it shelters in the shade. It is extremely active and alert and an expert climber. It feeds on insects such as flies and beetles, and on invertebrates such as earthworms, spiders, snails and slugs. A gregarious species, it lives in small colonies.

Soon after their winter hibernation, the lizards mate, males competing with one another for females. The female digs a hole and lays 2 to 10 eggs which she covers with soil. The eggs hatch in 2 to 3 months. In a warm spring, with good food supplies, wall lizards may lay several clutches.

NAME: Bosc's Fringe-toed Lizard, *Acanthodactylus boskianus*
RANGE: Egypt, Saudi Arabia
HABITAT: desert
SIZE: 12.5 cm (5 in)

A sand-coloured, desert-living lizard, this species has long toes bordered with broad combs of scales; this enlarges the surface area of the feet and thus improves the grip on the sand. It can run quickly over sand and digs deep burrows for refuge. The female lays 2 to 4 eggs which she buries in a hole she digs in the sand.

NAME: Algerian Sand Racer, *Psammodromus algirus*
RANGE: Spain, Portugal, S. W. France, N. Africa
HABITAT: dense vegetation in sandy areas, woodland, gardens, parks
SIZE: 30 cm (11¾ in)

The reptile most commonly seen in urban areas within its range, the sand racer is metallic brown, with light stripes down its sides. Its tail is long and stiff and often orange-coloured in juveniles. In the morning, the sand racer is sluggish while it basks in the sun after the cool night. When warmed up, it is an agile, fast-moving lizard which hunts for invertebrate prey among vegetation or on the ground.

The female sand racer lays 6 or more eggs which hatch in about 2 months.

NAME: Race-runner, *Eremias* sp.
RANGE: Europe, central Asia to Mongolia; Africa
HABITAT: desert, semi-arid scrub, grassland, rocky desert
SIZE: 15–22 cm (6–8½ in)

There are many species of *Eremias* lizards, many not yet properly classified. Most have scaly bodies and well-developed legs and are marked with spots, arranged in rows along the body. They tend to live in dry areas, taking refuge among rocks and in crevices, and feed on invertebrates, mainly insects and spiders.

Some *Eremias* lizards reproduce by laying clutches of 2 to 12 eggs, but others give birth to living young.

NAME: Essex's Mountain Lizard, *Tropidosaura essexi*
RANGE: South Africa
HABITAT: mountains
SIZE: 14 cm (5½ in)

A small lizard with a blunt, rounded snout, Essex's mountain lizard is marked with pale stripes, running from behind its head down its body and on to its tail. A ground-dweller, it is active in the daytime and is quick and agile in its movements. It feeds on insects and small invertebrates.

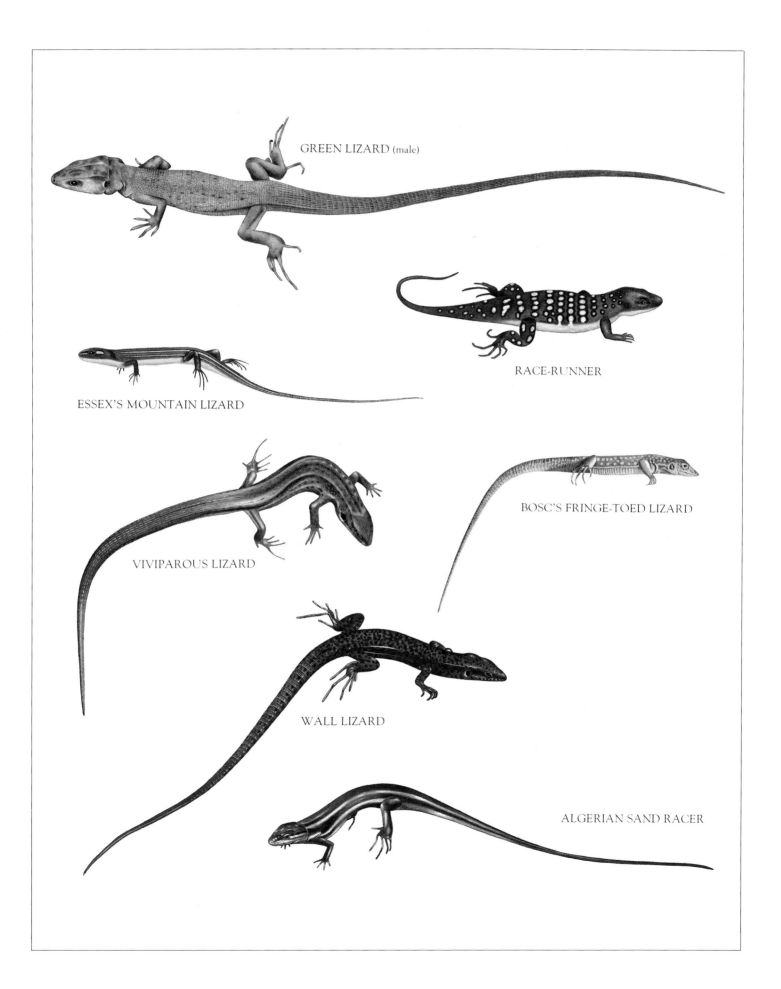

GREEN LIZARD (male)

RACE-RUNNER

ESSEX'S MOUNTAIN LIZARD

BOSC'S FRINGE-TOED LIZARD

VIVIPAROUS LIZARD

WALL LIZARD

ALGERIAN SAND RACER

Girdled and Plated Lizards

NAME: *Cordylosaurus subtessellatus*
RANGE: Africa: S. Angola, Namibia
HABITAT: dry, rocky areas
SIZE: 15 cm (6 in)

The greatly compressed head and body of this lizard make it easy for it to take refuge in crevices and crannies in the rocks, where it hides from enemies or shelters from intense heat or night-time cold. It may also shelter under stones. In each lower eyelid there is a transparent "window", so that the lizard can close its eyes in windy weather, when sand and dust might blow into them, but is still able to see. Under its digits are keeled scales, perhaps to help it grip on rocks. Its tail is easily shed and regenerated.

An agile, ground-dwelling lizard, it feeds on insects and other small invertebrates. The female reproduces by laying eggs.

NAME: Imperial Flat Lizard, *Platysaurus imperator*
RANGE: Africa: N. E. Zimbabwe, contiguous Mozambique
HABITAT: rocky knolls of granite and sandstone in grassland
SIZE: 39 cm (15¼ in)

The head, body, limbs and tail of this lizard are all flattened laterally; in consequence it can take refuge in narrow cracks and crevices in the rocks among which it lives. As these rocky knolls weather, many crevices are formed, ideal as hiding places; once in a crevice, the lizard expands its body with air and braces itself against the rock, making it virtually impossible for any predator to remove it. This lizard tends to frequent the tops of the knolls, whereas the other platysaurans live at the base.

The biggest species in its genus, the imperial flat lizard has large scales on its neck and a smooth back. The male, with his yellow, red and black body, is larger and more brightly coloured than the female, which is largely black, with three distinctive yellow stripes on her head that taper off toward the back. Males hold territories which they compete for and defend against intruders by adopting an aggressive posture, rearing up and displaying throat and chest colours. Active in the daytime, flat lizards hunt insects, particularly locusts and beetles. They shelter from the midday heat and emerge again to hunt in the afternoon.

The female flat lizard lays 2 eggs, elongate in shape, in a crevice in the rocks.

CORDYLIDAE:
Girdled and Plated Lizard Family

The cordylid lizards are an African family of about 40 species, found largely in rocky or arid habitats, south of the Sahara and in Madagascar. Names include plated, whip, girdled, crag, snake and flat lizards, which gives some idea of the range of adaptations within the family.

The typical cordylid lizard has a body covered with bony plates which underlie the external and visible scales. This undercoat of armour, however, is not continuous over the whole body: on each side there is a lateral groove, without a plate layer, which allows body expansion, when the belly is full of food for example, or, in egg-laying females, when distended with eggs. There are many variations of form within the family: the girdle-tailed lizards have short tails, armoured with rings of spines, and often have spines on the head; flat lizards of the genus *Platysaurus* have flattened bodies and skin covered with smooth granules; snake lizards of the genus *Chamaesaura* are very elongate, with tails up to three-quarters of their body length. Some cordylids have well-developed limbs, while in others the limbs are much reduced or even absent.

Most lizards in the family feed on insects and small invertebrates such as millipedes. Some of the larger forms also consume smaller lizards, and others are almost entirely vegetarian in their habits. Their reproductive habits vary, some species laying eggs and others bearing live young.

NAME: Transvaal Snake Lizard, *Chamaesaura aena*
RANGE: South Africa
HABITAT: grassland
SIZE: 40 cm (15¾ in)

This snakelike lizard has an elongate body and a tail which is about three-quarters of its total length. It has four small limbs, each with five clawed digits; the other 3 species in this genus have at most two digits per limb, and one species, *C. macrolepsis*, has no front limbs at all. Active in the daytime, it moves quickly through the grass with serpentine undulations of its body, often with its head and forelimbs lifted off the ground. It feeds on insects, spiders, earthworms and other small invertebrates.

The female's 2 to 4 young develop inside her oviduct. The fully formed young break from their soft shells as they are expelled from her body.

NAME: Armadillo Lizard, *Cordylus cataphractus*
RANGE: South Africa: W. Cape Province
HABITAT: arid rocky areas
SIZE: 21 cm (8¼ in)

The armadillo lizard is heavily armoured, with strong spiny scales which extend from its head right along its back and tail. Its head, body and clublike tail are all flattened, enabling it to wriggle easily into rock crevices for shelter. The nostrils are elongated into little tubes.

A ground-dwelling lizard, it is active in the daytime and feeds on a wide variety of insects, as well as on spiders and other invertebrates. It is fairly slow-moving and, rather than darting for cover when threatened, may adopt a curious defensive posture which earns it its common name. It rolls itself up like an armadillo, its tail tightly held in its jaws; thus presenting a spiny ring to the predator and protecting the softer, vulnerable belly area.

The 1 to 3 young of the armadillo lizard develop inside the female's body. The tiny, fully formed lizards break from their soft membranous shells as they are expelled from her body.

NAME: Plated Lizard, *Gerrhosaurus flavigularis*
RANGE: Africa: Sudan, Ethiopia, south through E. Africa to South Africa: Cape Province
HABITAT: grassland, scrub
SIZE: 45.5 cm (18 in)

A ground-living and burrowing lizard, this species is usually greenish-grey or brownish, with a red or yellow throat and often a narrow stripe down each side. It is well armoured, with hard body plates, and head shields fused to the skull. The tail is generally about two-thirds of the total length. Its limbs are well developed and it has five toes on each foot. These are not specially adapted for digging, and the lizard probably does most of its tunnelling after rain when the ground is soft. Active by day, it hunts insects and is rarely seen, despite its size. It moves rapidly through the grass and at any sign of danger darts into its burrow, usually positioned under a bush.

The female plated lizard lays clutches of 4 or 5 eggs in a shallow pit which she excavates.

NAME: Girdled Lizard, *Zonosaurus* sp.
RANGE: Madagascar
HABITAT: forest
SIZE: 38–61 cm (15–24 in)

There are 3 *Zonosaurus* species, all large, strong, ground-dwelling lizards. They have well-developed limbs and distinct grooves along their sides to allow for body expansion. Little is known of their habits or biology.

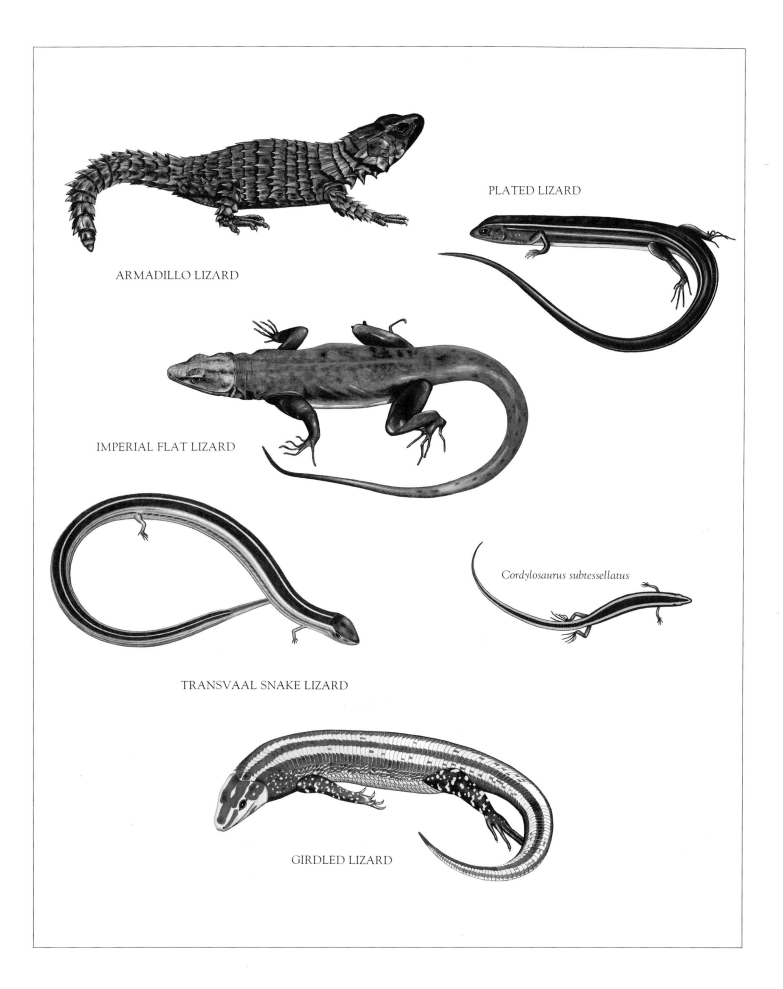

PLATED LIZARD

ARMADILLO LIZARD

IMPERIAL FLAT LIZARD

Cordylosaurus subtessellatus

TRANSVAAL SNAKE LIZARD

GIRDLED LIZARD

Old World Burrowing Lizards, Slow Worms, Legless Lizards

DIBAMIDAE: Old World Burrowing Lizard Family

This small family contains only 3 species of small, wormlike, limbless lizards, all in the genus *Dibamus*. They live in parts of Southeast Asia, the Philippines and New Guinea.

NAME: *Dibamus novaeguineae*
RANGE: New Guinea
HABITAT: forest
SIZE: up to 30 cm (11¾ in)

All three *Dibamus* species are blind, limbless lizards, specialized for a burrowing, underground life. The body is wormlike and the eyes and ears are covered by skin. The nostrils are positioned on an enlarged scale at the tip of the snout, and the teeth are small and backward curving. The male has stumplike vestiges of hind limbs that are used for clasping the female when mating. Dibamids will burrow into rotting logs as well as soil.

Little is known of their habits. Eggs, which were probably dibamid eggs, have been discovered in rotting logs and forest floor humus.

ANGUIDAE: Slow Worm and Alligator Lizard Family

There are about 80 species in this family of elongate, snakelike lizards, found in North, Central and South America, the West Indies, Europe, North Africa and Asia. Typically, they have smooth, elongate bodies and tails, movable eyelids and external ear openings. Most are land-dwelling or burrowing animals and many, such as the slow worms and glass lizards and snakes, are limbless or have only vestigial limbs. The alligator lizards of North and Central America, however, have well-developed limbs.

Many of these lizards have stiff bodies, armoured by bony plates under the surface skin. In order that their bodies can expand when breathing, or to accommodate food or eggs, there are grooves of soft scales along their sides. Their long tails easily become detached if seized by an attacker, usually along one of the series of fracture planes. The tail is regrown in a few weeks, but not always completely.

Most anguids feed on insects, small invertebrates and even small mammals and lizards. All but a few species reproduce by laying eggs. The others, mostly species found at high altitudes, give birth to live young.

NAME: Galliwasp, *Diploglossus lessorae*
RANGE: Central America, N. South America
HABITAT: forest
SIZE: up to 35 cm (13¾ in)

The smooth, shiny galliwasp resembles the alligator lizards but has a more elongate body and lacks the expandable grooves along the sides of the body that the heavily armoured alligator lizards possess. It is a ground-dwelling species, active in the daytime, and feeds on insects, worms and molluscs. It is believed to reproduce by laying eggs.

NAME: Southern Alligator Lizard, *Gerrhonotus multicarinatus*
RANGE: W. USA: Washington; Baja California
HABITAT: grassland, open woodland
SIZE: 25.5–43 cm (10–17 in)

The agile southern alligator lizard has a strong prehensile tail, which it can wrap around branches and use like a fifth limb when climbing in bushes. There are 5 subspecies of this lizard, which vary in coloration from reddish-brown to yellowish-grey, usually with some dark markings, but all have distinct folds along their sides, where flexible scales allow the stiff, armoured body to expand. These lizards are active in the daytime, when they hunt for insects and any other small creatures that they are able to catch and swallow, including scorpions and black widow spiders.

Alligator lizards breed in the summer, females laying several clutches over the season. There are usually 12 eggs in a clutch, but there may be up to 40 on occasion.

NAME: Glass Snake, *Ophisaurus apodus*
RANGE: Europe: Yugoslavia, Greece to Black Sea region, east to S.W. and central Asia
SIZE: up to 1.2 m (4 ft)

The largest species of its family, the glass snake is a heavy-bodied, snakelike animal with vestiges of hind limbs. The body is rather stiff, with a bony layer under the smooth scales. Grooves of flexible scales on each side allow the body to expand when necessary. The glass snake is active in the daytime and at dawn and dusk, feeding on lizards, mice and other small animals which it kills with its powerful jaws.

Males become aggressive and competitive in the breeding season and there is fierce rivalry for mates. The female lays 5 to 7 eggs in a hollow under a rock or log, or in a pile of rotting vegetation. She curls around her eggs and guards them from predators while they incubate. The young hatch in about 4 weeks and are about 12.5 cm (5 in) long.

NAME: Slow Worm, *Anguis fragilis*
RANGE: Europe (not Ireland, S. Spain and Portugal or N. Scandinavia), east to central and S. W. Asia; N. W. Africa
HABITAT: fields, meadows, scrub, heath, up to 2,400 m (7,900 ft)
SIZE: 35–54 cm (13¾–21¼ in)

The slow worm is a smooth, extremely snakelike creature with no visible limbs. It is reddish-brown, brown or grey above; females usually have a dark stripe on the back, while some males may have blue spots. It moves by serpentine undulations and can shed its long tail if seized by an enemy. The tail does not fully regenerate, however, and is then stumplike. The night and heat of the day are spent under rocks or logs, and the slow worm emerges in the morning and evening to hunt for slugs and worms, as well as spiders, insects and larvae. It is slower-moving than most lizards but can disappear into cover with considerable speed.

In late spring, breeding males become aggressive and compete with one another for mates. As they copulate, the male holds the female's neck or head in his jaws. About 3 months later, the female gives birth to live young, usually 6 to 12 but sometimes as many as 20. The young develop in thin-shelled eggs inside her body and break out of the membranous shells as they are laid. They are about 6 to 9 cm (2¼ to 3½ in) long at birth.

ANNIELLIDAE: California Legless Lizard Family

There are only 2 species of these slender, wormlike, burrowing lizards, found only in the USA and Mexico. They are similar to the anguid lizards but lack the bony plates under the skin and have no external ear openings.

NAME: California Legless Lizard, *Anniella pulchra*
RANGE: USA: California; Mexico, Baja California
HABITAT: beaches, sand-dunes, banks of streams, soft loamy soil
SIZE: 15–23 cm (6–9 in)

Specialized for burrowing, this legless lizard has a smooth body, which helps it to move easily through soil, and a shovel-shaped snout for digging. Its eyes are small and have movable lids. Most of its life is spent underground or burrowing in leaf litter, searching for insects and insect larvae. It rarely moves in the open. One race of this species, *A. pulchra nigra*, is in danger of extinction.

These lizards are live-bearing; females produce litters of up to 4 fully formed young.

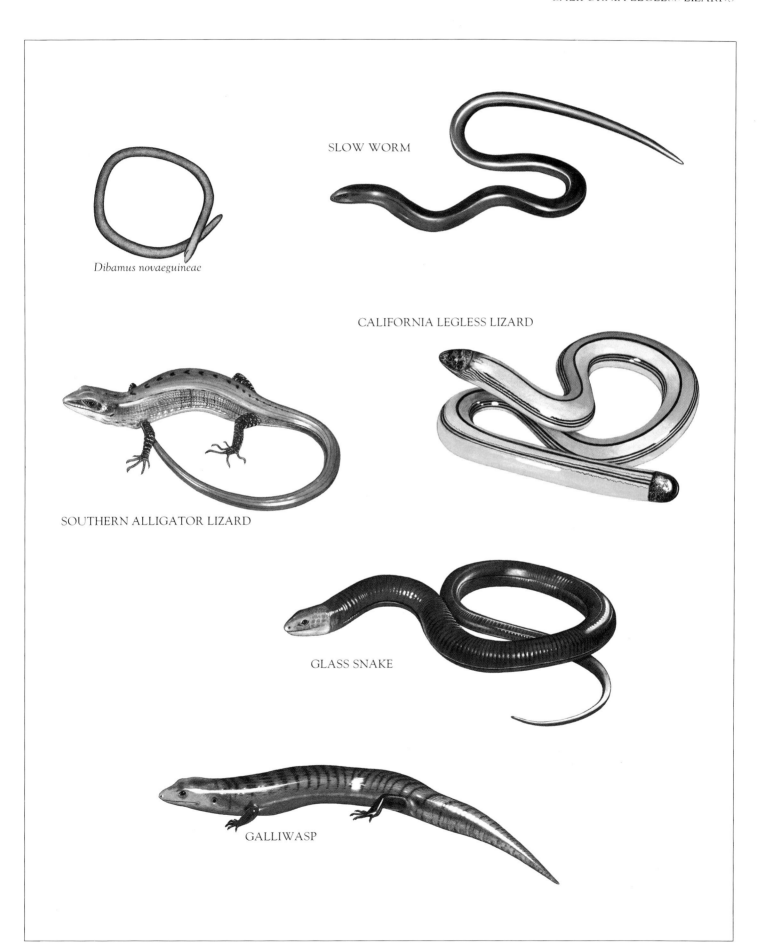

SLOW WORM

Dibamus novaeguineae

CALIFORNIA LEGLESS LIZARD

SOUTHERN ALLIGATOR LIZARD

GLASS SNAKE

GALLIWASP

Crocodile Lizards, Gila Monster, Monitors

XENOSAURIDAE:
Crocodile Lizard Family

There are 4 species in this family, 3 in Central America and Mexico and 1 in south China. They are related to the anguid lizards and, under the body scales, have bony plates, which may be tiny or large but are not joined together. Unlike many anguids, however, their limbs are well developed.

NAME: *Xenosaurus* sp.
RANGE: **Mexico, Guatemala**
HABITAT: **rain forest**
SIZE: **about 20 cm (7¾ in)**

These powerful, strong-limbed lizards have flat heads and robust bodies. They are inconspicuous creatures and are not often seen, spending much of their time in refuges beneath tree roots or in rocky crevices. They will also lie in water for long periods. Active at night, they feed on insects, particularly winged termites and ants. If alarmed, *Xenosaurus* adopts a threat posture, with mouth agape, revealing a black membrane.

The females gives birth to litters of 3 fully formed live young which are about 4 cm (1½ in) long at birth.

VARANIDAE:
Monitor Lizard Family

The monitor lizards of the Old World include within their number the largest of lizards. The komodo dragon may be 3 m (10 ft) long and weigh 163 kg (360 lb); several other species exceed 2 m (6½ ft) in length. There are about 30 species of monitor in a single genus, all of them elongate lizards with long necks and tails and well-developed limbs. Their snakelike forked tongues can be retracted into the mouth.

Monitors occur in Africa (except Madagascar), the Middle East, southern Asia, Indonesia and Australasia. All are voracious carnivores. Male monitor lizards may perform spectacular ritualized fights to assert their dominance. They rear up on their hind legs and wrestle with their forelimbs until one contestant is pushed over and defeated. Monitors reproduce by laying eggs, and several species are known to dig pits in the ground in which the eggs are buried to incubate.

NAME: **Komodo Dragon,** *Varanus komodensis*
RANGE: **islands of Komodo, Flores, Pintja and Padar, east of Java**
HABITAT: **grassland**
SIZE: **3 m (10 ft)**   Ⓡ

The awe-inspiring komodo dragon dwarfs most present-day lizards. It has a heavy body, long thick tail and well-developed limbs with talonlike claws. Its teeth are large and jagged and it has a forked tongue that can be flicked in and out of the mouth. Despite its size, it is a good climber, moves surprisingly quickly and swims well; it tends to live near water. It is active during the day and preys on animals as large as hog deer and wild boar, as well as on small deer and pigs.

The female komodo lays about 15 eggs which she buries in the ground.

NAME: **Nile Monitor,** *Varanus niloticus*
RANGE: **Africa: south and east of the Sahara to Cape Province**
HABITAT: **forest, open country**
SIZE: **over 2 m (6½ ft)**

The versatile, yet unspecialized, Nile monitor is a robust, strong reptile, typical of the monitor group. Using its broad tail as a rudder, it swims and dives well and can climb trees with the aid of its huge claws and strong prehensile tail, which it uses to hold on to branches. It can also dig burrows. Nile monitors tend to stay near water and do not venture into desert areas. They feed on frogs, fish and snails, as well as on crocodile eggs and young.

One of the most prolific egg-laying lizards, the female Nile monitor lays up to 60 eggs in a termite mound. She tears a hole in the wall, lays her eggs inside and departs. The termites repair their nest, thus enclosing the eggs in the warm, safe termitarium. When they hatch, the young monitors must make their own way out of the nest.

NAME: **Gould's Monitor,** *Varanus gouldi*
RANGE: **Australia**
HABITAT: **coastal forest to sandy desert**
SIZE: **about 1.5 m (5 ft)**

The widespread Gould's monitor, also known as the sand monitor, varies in size, coloration and pattern over its range. Like those of all monitors, its limbs are powerful, and its distinctly ridged tail is laterally compressed, except at the base. It is ground-dwelling, sheltering in burrows, which it digs or takes over from other animals, or under logs and debris. To find food, it must roam over large areas of sparsely populated country, searching for birds, mammals, reptiles, insects, even carrion. Like all monitors, the female reproduces by laying eggs.

HELODERMATIDAE:
Gila Monster Family

There are only 2 species in this family, which is related to the monitor lizards and the rare, earless monitor. They are the gila monster, from western North America, and the Mexican beaded lizard.

NAME: **Gila Monster,** *Heloderma suspectum*
RANGE: **S.W. USA: S. Utah, Arizona to New Mexico; Mexico**
HABITAT: **arid and semi-arid areas with some vegetation**
SIZE: **45–61 cm (17¾–24 in)**   Ⓥ

This formidable, heavy-bodied lizard has a short, usually stout tail, in which it can store fat for use in periods of food shortage. It is gaudily patterned and has brightly coloured beadlike scales on its back. The gila lives on the ground and shelters under rocks or in a burrow, which it digs itself or takes over from another animal. It is primarily nocturnal but may emerge during the day in spring.

The two members of the gila monster family are the only venomous lizards. The venom is produced in glands in the lower jaw and enters the mouth via grooved teeth at the front of the lower jaw; it flows into the victim as the lizard chews. The gila also eats the eggs of birds and reptiles.

Gila monsters mate in the summer, and the female lays 3 to 5 eggs some time later, in the autumn or winter.

LANTHANOTIDAE:
Earless Monitor Family

The earless monitor, found only in Sarawak, is the only species in its family. Little is known of the biology of this rare, nocturnal lizard.

NAME: **Earless Monitor,** *Lanthanotus borneensis*
RANGE: **Sarawak**
HABITAT: **forest**
SIZE: **up to 43 cm (17 in)**

The earless monitor has an elongate, rather flattened body and short but strong limbs, each with five digits. On each body scale there is a small tubercle. Its eyes are tiny with movable lids, the lower of which have transparent "windows", and there are no external ear openings. Much of the earless monitor's life is spent burrowing underground or swimming; it avoids bright light and does not need intense warmth. In captivity the earless monitor will eat fish, but its natural diet is not known.

NILE MONITOR

KOMODO DRAGON

GOULD'S MONITOR

GILA MONSTER

Xenosaurus sp.

EARLESS MONITOR

Amphisbaenids

NAME: **Florida Worm Lizard,** *Rhineura floridana*
RANGE: **USA: N. and central Florida**
HABITAT: **sandy, wooded areas**
SIZE: **18–40.5 cm (7–16 in)**

The only blind, limbless lizard in North America, the Florida worm lizard is just over 0.5 cm (⅕ in) in diameter and has a shovel-shaped head. It lives underground, feeding on worms, spiders and termites, and rarely comes to the surface unless driven by rain or disturbed by cultivation. Unlike an earthworm, it leaves a tunnel behind it as it burrows, pushing through the earth with its spadelike snout and compacting the soil as it goes, to form the tunnel.

In summer, the Florida worm lizard lays up to 3 long, thin eggs in a burrow. The young hatch in autumn, when they are about 10 cm (4 in) long.

Fossil research has shown that this amphisbaenid was at one time widely distributed in North America.

NAME: **Two-legged Worm Lizard,** *Bipes biporus*
RANGE: **Mexico, Baja California**
HABITAT: **arid land**
SIZE: **20 cm (7¾ in)**

The worm lizards of this genus are the only members of the family to possess limbs. They have two tiny front legs with five clawed toes on each limb. Despite their size, these limbs are powerful, and the digits are adapted for digging and climbing. Like all amphisbaenids, the two-legged worm lizard spends most of its life underground in burrows and uses its limbs to start digging its tunnels. Once the burrow is begun, it pushes through with its round head, compacting the soil as it goes. When digging a large tunnel, it may use its limbs as well as its head.

These worm lizards feed on worms and termites. Although little is known of their breeding habits, they are believed to lay eggs.

NAME: **South African Shield Snout,** *Monopeltis capensis*
RANGE: **Africa: central South Africa, Zimbabwe**
HABITAT: **sandy soil**
SIZE: **30 cm (11¾ in)**

The thick horny plates on the shovel-like head of this amphisbaenid enable it to burrow into harder soils than many other species. It tunnels down to depths of 20 cm (7¾ in) and only emerges above ground when driven by rains or if attacked by ants. When they do emerge, shield snouts are preyed on by birds such as ravens and kites. Shield snouts themselves feed on termites, beetles and other ground-living insects.

AMPHISBAENIDAE: Amphisbaenid Family

The 100 or so species of amphisbaenids are extraordinary, wormlike, burrowing reptiles, whose position in the reptile group is not fully understood. Known as worm lizards, they are not true lizards and are given their own suborder within the Squamata order, on a parallel with the much larger lizard and snake groups. Most species occur in Central and South America and Africa, but there are a few species in the warmer parts of North America and Europe. They prefer moist habitats in which they can build semi-permanent tunnel systems that will not collapse after the animal has passed through. They quickly dehydrate in dry soil. Water is taken into the mouth and swallowed, not absorbed through the skin as was once believed.

Most species are limbless, only the 3 species in the genus *Bipes* have tiny forelimbs. The skin is loosely attached over the simple cylindrical body, which is ringed with small scales. The tail is pointed in some species and rounded in others but is always covered with horny scales. Amphisbaenids have no external ear openings, and their tiny eyes are covered with scales.

Amphisbaenids live underground in burrows which they dig themselves, often near ant or termite colonies. Bracing their long bodies against the walls of the tunnel, they excavate new lengths by repeated battering strokes of their hard, strong heads. Like worms, they can move backward or forward in a straight line with no body undulations; ideal for life in tunnels. Indeed, the Greek word *amphisbaena* means "goes both ways". This ability, combined with the similar appearance of the head and tail, has caused many to see the amphisbaenid as a two-headed monster, and it is mentioned as such in a Roman epic poem.

Amphisbaenids find all their prey — mostly insects and worms — below ground. Larger species may also attack and eat small vertebrate animals. They are able to hear their prey crawling in the ground and move accurately in its direction. The sense of smell also seems to play a part in locating prey. Once it has found its quarry, the amphisbaenid grabs it and tears it apart with its strong, interlocking teeth, set in powerful jaws.

Little is known of the breeding habits of amphisbaenids, but most species are believed to lay eggs which incubate and hatch in their underground burrows.

NAME: **White-bellied Worm Lizard,** *Amphisbaena alba*
RANGE: **tropical South America; Trinidad**
HABITAT: **rain forest**
SIZE: **61 cm (24 in)**

The body of this worm lizard, the most widespread in South America, is cylindrical over its entire length, the tail being almost as thick and blunt as the head. Tail and head look similar, and the species is known as the two-headed blind snake in some areas. It is over 2.5 cm (1 in) in diameter.

Although a burrowing, underground animal, this species often crawls over the forest floor, particularly after heavy rain. It feeds on earthworms and ants and is often found in ants' nests. Indeed, some tribes call it "ant king" or "mother ant" and believe it to be reared by ants. If in danger, this worm lizard lifts its tail and moves it around as if it were a head. Presumably this tricks the enemy into attacking the tail, thus keeping the vulnerable head area safe and enabling the worm lizard to make a counter-attack.

NAME: **Somali Edge Snout,** *Agamodon anguliceps*
RANGE: **Africa: Somali Republic, S. E. Ethiopia**
HABITAT: **sandy soil**
SIZE: **11 cm (4¼ in)**

The Somali edge snout has a shorter, thicker body than most amphisbaenids. Its tail is short and tapered, and its wedge-shaped head makes it a particularly efficient burrower, even in hard soils. On the front of its head it has a pair of sharp, vertical ridges, and by screwing motions of its specially adapted head, the edge snout excavates its tunnel and compacts the soil. At night, it moves up to within 5 to 7 cm (2 to 2¾ in) of the surface and, as the daytime temperature rises, descends again to depths of about 15 to 30 cm (6 to 11¾ in). It occasionally moves above ground, swinging its head from side to side and pulling itself along.

NAME: **Worm Lizard,** *Blanus cinereus*
RANGE: **Spain, Portugal, N. W. Africa**
HABITAT: **sandy soil or humus, often in woodland**
SIZE: **22–30 cm (8½–11¾ in)**

The only European amphisbaenid, this worm lizard has a small, pointed head and a tapering tail. It spends most of its life in underground burrows and is only rarely seen above ground except after heavy rain or when it is disturbed by cultivation. It feeds on small invertebrates, particularly ants.

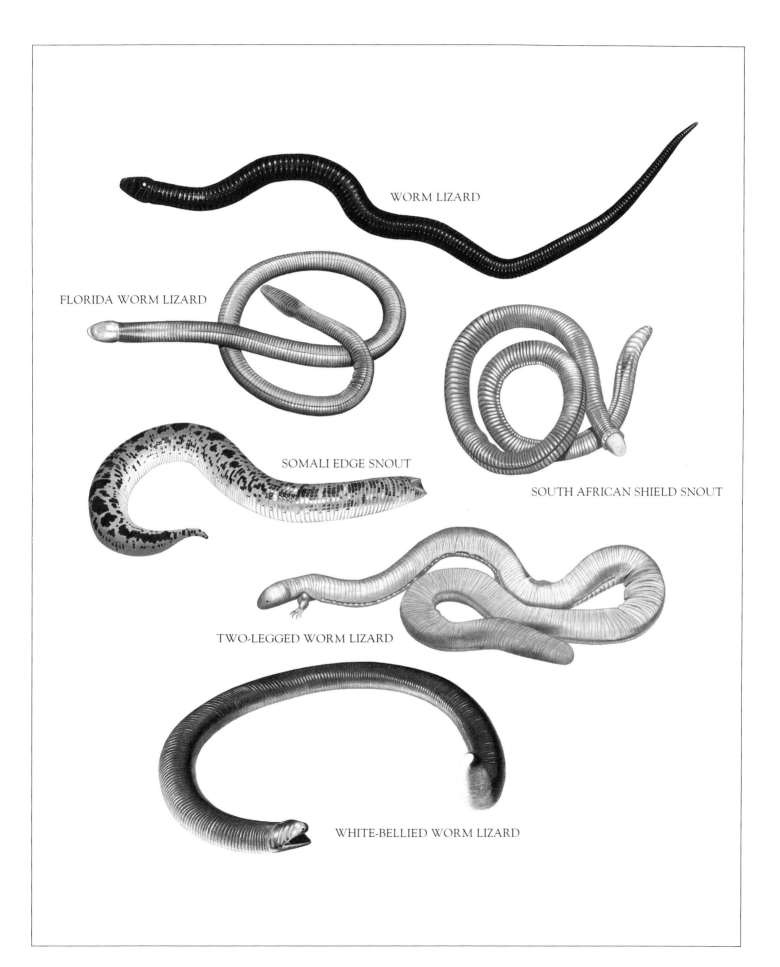

WORM LIZARD

FLORIDA WORM LIZARD

SOMALI EDGE SNOUT

SOUTH AFRICAN SHIELD SNOUT

TWO-LEGGED WORM LIZARD

WHITE-BELLIED WORM LIZARD

Thread Snakes, Blind Snakes, Pipe Snakes, Shieldtail Snakes, Sunbeam Snake

LEPTOTYPHLOPIDAE:
Thread Snake Family

The thread snakes are small, worm-shaped, burrowing snakes that grow to about 38 cm (15 in) long. They possess minute vestiges of a pelvic girdle and hind limbs, and their tiny rudimentary eyes are hidden beneath scales. Like their relatives in the families Typhlopidae and Anomalepidae, these snakes are specialized for their burrowing existence and, in one feature in particular, have evolved in a way which is dramatically different from all other snakes. The size of the mouth has become reduced, and it is only about half the length of the head, whereas in most snakes the mouth is as large as possible in order to accommodate a variety of sizeable prey.

Thread snakes feed on termites and ants. The approximately 50 species live in Africa, tropical Asia and southern USA, through Central and South America to Argentina.

NAME: **Western Blind Snake,** *Leptotyphlops humilis*
RANGE: **S. W. USA: S. W. Utah, south to N. Mexico and Baja California**
HABITAT: **desert, grassland, scrub, rocky canyons**
SIZE: **18–38 cm (7–15 in)**

A smooth, round-bodied snake, the western blind snake has a blunt head and tail. It lives almost anywhere where there is sandy or gravelly soil suitable for burrowing, and spends much of its life below ground, occasionally emerging at dusk on warm evenings or on overcast days. It feeds on ants and termites which it locates by smell and, with its slender body, can enter right into their nests.

The snakes mate in spring and the female lays 2 to 6 eggs. She watches over the eggs, which may be laid in a communal nest.

TYPHLOPIDAE:
Blind Snake Family

The 180 species in this family of burrowing snakes occur in tropical and warm temperate regions throughout the world. They rarely exceed 60 cm (23½ in) in length. Well adapted for burrowing, they have thin, cylindrical bodies, smooth, polished scales and narrow, streamlined heads. Their eyes are extremely small and each is covered with a translucent scale. They feed on small invertebrates, particularly ants.

NAME: **Schlegel's Blind Snake,** *Typhlops schlegelii*
RANGE: **Africa: Kenya to South Africa**
HABITAT: **sandy or loamy soil**
SIZE: **60 cm (23½ in)**

Schlegel's blind snake has a spine on the end of its tail which helps to provide leverage when it is burrowing. Although most of its life is spent underground, it will come near the surface in damp or wet weather.

The female lays 12 to 60 eggs, which are already well advanced in their development when they are laid and take only 4 to 6 weeks to hatch.

ANOMALEPIDAE

Sometimes grouped in the Typhlopidae family, there are about 20 species in this family, all found in Central and South America. They closely resemble the blind and thread snakes.

NAME: *Anomalepis* **sp.**
RANGE: **Mexico, tropical Central and South America to Peru**
HABITAT: **forest**
SIZE: **up to 40 cm (15¾ in)**

There are 4 species of *Anomalepis* snakes, all little-known wormlike burrowers with cylindrical bodies. They spend much of their lives buried under leaf litter in damp humus and are rarely seen on the surface, except after rain. They feed on termites, ants and other small invertebrates.

ANILIIDAE: Pipe Snake Family

There are 10 species in this family, all of which have a variety of primitive characteristics, including a pelvis and vestigial hind limbs, which appear as spurs, close to the vent. One species lives in northern South America and the other 9 are found in Southeast Asia. All are excellent burrowers and feed on vertebrates such as other snakes.

NAME: **False Coral Snake,** *Anilius scytale*
RANGE: **N. South America, east of Andes**
HABITAT: **forest**
SIZE: **75–85 cm (29½–33½ in)**

A burrowing species, the false coral snake has a cylindrical body, small head and smooth scales. Its tiny eyes lie beneath transparent scales. Its small mouth is not particularly flexible and it is restricted to slender prey animals such as other snakes, caecilians (limbless wormlike amphibians) and the snakelike amphisbaenids.

The female's young develop inside her body and are born fully formed.

UROPELTIDAE:
Shieldtail Snake Family

There are about 40 species in this family of burrowing snakes, all found in India and Sri Lanka.

NAME: **Red-blotched Shieldtail,** *Uropeltis biomaculatus*
RANGE: **India, Sri Lanka**
HABITAT: **mountain forest**
SIZE: **up to 30.5 cm (12 in)**

The red-blotched shieldtail has the typical cylindrical body of a burrowing snake. It tunnels by forming the body into a series of S-bends, which press against the sides of the tunnel, and then thrusting the head forward into the soil. It is a secretive, inoffensive snake and feeds mainly on earthworms and grubs.

The female gives birth to 3 to 8 fully formed live young, which have developed inside her body and hatch from their membranous shells as they are laid.

NAME: **Blyth's Landau Shieldtail,** *Rhinophis blythis*
RANGE: **Sri Lanka**
HABITAT: **forest**
SIZE: **up to 35.5 cm (14 in)**

This small shieldtail burrows through the soil in the same manner as the red-blotched shieldtail. Most of its life is spent beneath the ground and it feeds on earthworms. Males tend to have longer tails than females. The female gives birth to litters of 3 to 6 fully formed live young which are about 1 cm (⅜ in) long at birth.

XENOPELTIDAE:
Sunbeam Snake Family

Placed in a family of its own, the sunbeam snake of Southeast Asia has both primitive and advanced features. Although much of its skull structure is primitive and inflexible, its lower jaw is flexible, which permits a more varied diet. Like the more advanced snakes, it has no pelvic girdle.

NAME: **Sunbeam Snake,** *Xenopeltis unicolor*
RANGE: **S. E. Asia: Burma to Indonesia**
HABITAT: **rice fields, cultivated land**
SIZE: **up to 1 m (3¼ ft)**

The iridescence of its smooth, blue scales gives the sunbeam snake its name. It spends time both above and below ground and, using its head, can burrow rapidly in soft soil. With its flexible lower jaw, it is able to take a wide range of fair-sized prey, including frogs, small rodents and birds.

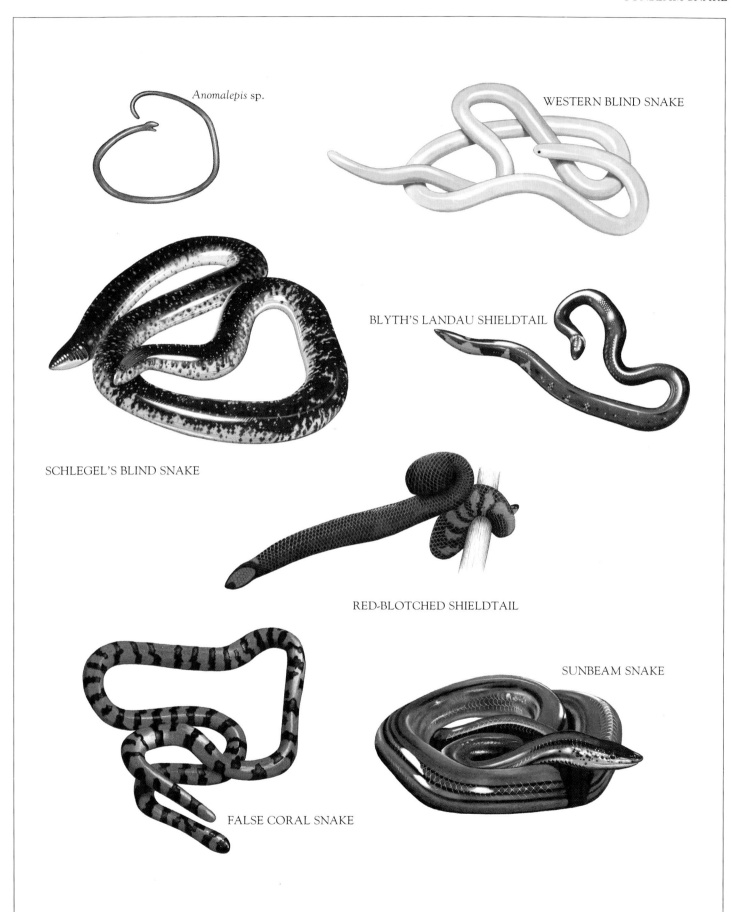

Anomalepis sp.

WESTERN BLIND SNAKE

BLYTH'S LANDAU SHIELDTAIL

SCHLEGEL'S BLIND SNAKE

RED-BLOTCHED SHIELDTAIL

SUNBEAM SNAKE

FALSE CORAL SNAKE

Pythons and Boas, Wart Snakes

BOIDAE: Python and Boa Family

There are about 90 species of snake in this family, many of them well known. Most specialists regard the group as a primitive one, since its members retain characteristics which are found in lizards but which have been lost by the more highly evolved, advanced snakes, such as vipers. For example, a pelvic girdle and diminutive hind limbs are discernible in some species, and all possess two working lungs, while in advanced snakes the left lung has disappeared in the interests of streamlining.

With the family are 2 groups: the pythons and the boas. The 20 species of python inhabit the more tropical parts of the Old World. They are often found in or near water but also spend much of their time in trees and may have prehensile tails. They reproduce by laying eggs which develop and hatch outside the body. The boas are found mainly in the New World and live on the ground, in trees or in or near water. They produce live young which develop inside the body and hatch out of thin-shelled eggs as the eggs are laid.

All boid snakes are predators, but they are non-venomous, capturing their prey with their teeth or killing it by constriction — wrapping the prey in the powerful body coils until it suffocates.

NAME: **Emerald Tree Boa**, *Boa caninus*
RANGE: **South America: Guyana, south to Brazil and Bolivia**
HABITAT: **rain forest**
SIZE: **1.2 m (4 ft)**

This brilliantly coloured boa spends much of its life in trees, where it rests with its body flattened and pressed to a branch which it grasps with its prehensile tail. From this vantage point, it watches for prey, often birds and bats, which it catches and kills with its strong front teeth. It is the fastest-moving of all boas and is also a good swimmer.

NAME: **Boa Constrictor**, *Constrictor constrictor*
RANGE: **Mexico, Central and South America to N. Argentina; West Indies**
HABITAT: **desert to rain forest**
SIZE: **up to 5.6 m (18¼ ft)**

The second-largest snake in the Americas, the boa constrictor adapts to widely contrasting climatic conditions but seems to prefer swampy rain forest. Primarily a ground-living snake, it does, however, climb trees and has a slightly prehensile tail which allows it to grasp branches. It kills its prey, mostly birds and mammals, by encircling them in the muscular coils of its body until the prey is suffocated or crushed.

NAME: **Rubber Boa**, *Charina bottae*
RANGE: **W. USA: Washington to S. California, east to Montana and Utah**
HABITAT: **woodland, coniferous forest, meadows, sandy banks of streams**
SIZE: **35–84 cm (13¾–33 in)** Ⓡ

This small boa ranges farther into the temperate zone than any other. It varies in coloration from tan to olive-green, and the confusing appearance of its broad snout and blunt tail are the origin of its other common name of "two-headed snake".

Usually active in the evening and at night, it is a good burrower and swimmer and can climb, using its prehensile tail. During the day, it hides under rocks or logs, or burrows into sand or leaf litter. It feeds on small mammals, birds and lizards which it kills by constriction. In late summer, the female gives birth to 2 to 8 live young which measure 15 to 23 cm (6 to 9 in).

NAME: **Anaconda**, *Eunectes murinus*
RANGE: **South America, south to Argentina**
HABITAT: **swampy river valleys, stream banks**
SIZE: **9 m (29½ ft)**

One of the world's longest snakes, the anaconda spends much of its life in sluggish fresh water but also climbs small trees and bushes with the aid of its slightly prehensile tail. It does not pursue its prey but lurks in murky water, waiting for birds and animals to come to the edge to drink. It seizes its victim and then kills it by constriction. It can only remain submerged for about 10 minutes and usually glides along with the top of its head showing above the water.

In the breeding season, males court their mates by making loud booming sounds. Females produce litters of as many as 40 live young, each of which is about 66 cm (26 in) long at birth.

NAME: **Carpet Python**, *Morelia argus*
RANGE: **Australia, New Guinea**
HABITAT: **forest, scrub, bush**
SIZE: **3.4 m (11 ft)**

A common, widely distributed snake, the carpet python is usually found inland, less often on the coast. The dark patterning on its body mimics dead leaves and provides camouflage as it lurks among plant debris. It moves equally well on the ground, in trees or in water. Usually active at night, it rests during the day in a tree or hollow stump and occasionally basks in the sun. A non-venomous snake like all pythons, the carpet python kills small mammals, such as mice and rabbits, and birds, such as domestic fowl, with its sharp teeth. The female lays up to 35 eggs.

NAME: **Indian Python**, *Python molurus*
RANGE: **India, S.E. Asia, Indonesia**
HABITAT: **estuarine mangroves, scrub jungle, cool rain forest**
SIZE: **5–6.1 m (16½–20 ft)** Ⓥ

One of the largest species in the world, the Indian python has suffered a reduction in numbers in some areas where it is hunted for its fine skin. It is a thick-bodied, smooth snake with a head shaped like the head of a spear. Like others of its genus, it is believed to have heat sensors near the nostrils to help it find its warm-blooded prey. Coloration varies with locality, but the pale grey race found in west India is reputedly less irritable than others and is used by "snake-charmers".

During the day, the Indian python basks in the sun or rests in a cave, abandoned burrow or other refuge. At night it prowls around, looking for prey, or lies in wait at a water hole or other spot where it is sure to encounter its prey — mice, civets, small deer, wild boar and birds. It stalks the animal, then grasps and encircles it with its body coils, restricting the breathing and heartbeat until they fail.

The female python lays up to 100 eggs in a hole, cave or tree hollow and, coiling herself around the eggs, incubates them for 60 to 80 days. She occasionally makes rhythmic contractions of her body muscles, and by this gradual shuffling process can move the eggs to catch the warmth of the sun or the protection of the shade.

ACROCHORDIDAE: Wart Snake Family

The 2 species in this family are both aquatic, non-venomous snakes, found in India, Southeast Asia and Australia. They are most unusual, having loose, sagging skin and distinctly tapering bodies. Highly specialized for aquatic life, wart snakes have flaps in the roof of the mouth which close off the nasal passages when they are under water. In the same way, the notch on the upper lip, through which the sensory tongue is protruded, can be closed off by a pad on the chin.

NAME: **Elephant-trunk Snake**, *Acrochordus javanicus*
RANGE: **India, S.E. Asia, New Guinea**
HABITAT: **rivers, streams, canals**
SIZE: **1.5 m (5 ft)**

This stout, sluggish snake is almost helpless on land but an expert swimmer. It is generally more active at night and feeds exclusively on fish. The female gives birth to 25 to 30 live young which are active and able to feed immediately.

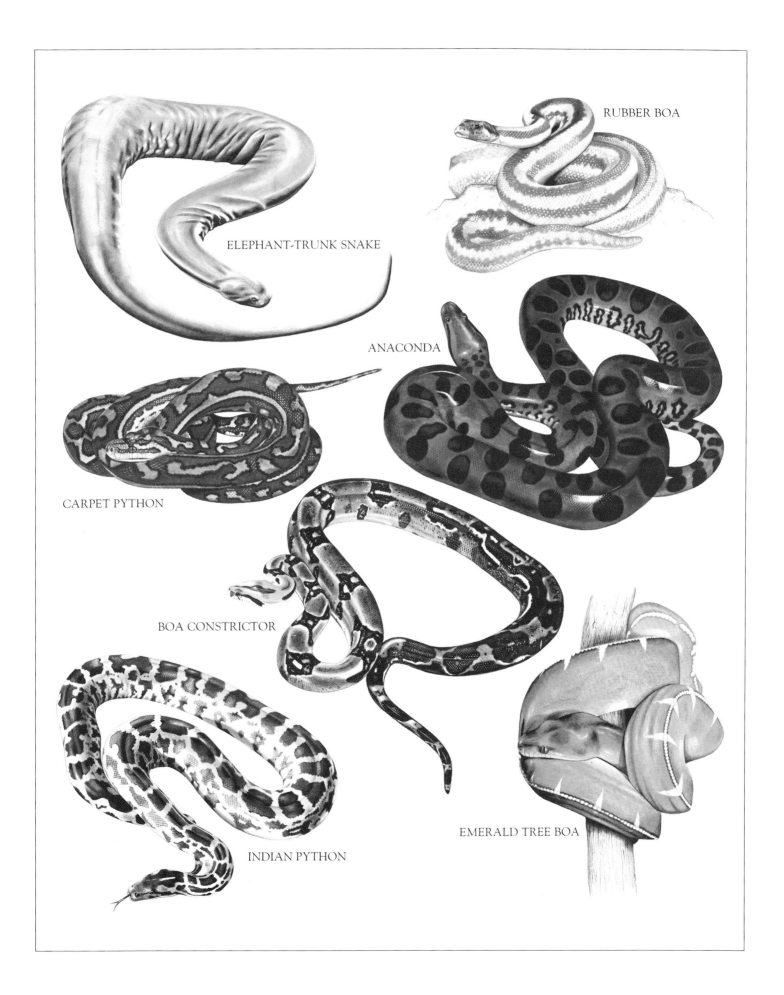

ELEPHANT-TRUNK SNAKE

RUBBER BOA

ANACONDA

CARPET PYTHON

BOA CONSTRICTOR

INDIAN PYTHON

EMERALD TREE BOA

Colubrine Snakes I

NAME: *Fimbrios klossi*
RANGE: South Vietnam, Kampuchea
HABITAT: mountains with low vegetation
SIZE: 40 cm (15¾ in)

This little-known snake is ground-dwelling and probably nocturnal. It has curious modifications of the scales around the mouth: they are curved, forming a fringe of soft projections the exact function of which is unknown, although they may be sensory. *Fimbrios* feeds mainly on earthworms.

Like other members of its subfamily, Xenodermatinae, *Fimbrios klossi* probably lays 2 to 4 eggs.

NAME: Slug Snake, *Pareas* sp.
RANGE: S. E. Asia
HABITAT: forest
SIZE: 30.5–76 cm (12–30 in)

The slug snakes, also known as blunt-heads, are mostly nocturnal and have slender bodies and short, wide heads. They feed mainly on slugs and snails, and their lower jaws are adapted for removing the snails from their shells, for they are capable of being extended and retracted independently of the upper jaws. Having seized a snail, the snake inserts its lower jaw into the shell so that the curved teeth at the tip of the jaw sink into the soft body. It then retracts its jaw, winkling out the snail from the shell.

These snakes lack the so-called mental groove on the chin possessed by most snakes that allows the jaw to be distended when taking in large prey. Thus their diet is restricted to the small items for which they are admirably specialized. As far as is known, these snakes reproduce by laying eggs.

NAME: Snail-eating Snake, *Dipsas indica*
RANGE: tropical South America
HABITAT: forest
SIZE: about 68 cm (26¾ in)

The snail-eating snake is a nocturnal, ground-dwelling species with a strong body, large head and blunt, short snout. Its upper jaw is short with few teeth, and its lower jaw long with elongate, curved teeth. The structure of the jaws is such that the lower jaw can be swung backward and forward without movement of the upper jaw.

It feeds entirely on snails in a manner similar to the *Pareas* snakes, inserting its lower jaw into the snail's shell, twisting it to sink the teeth into the soft body and then pulling it out. As it attempts to defend itself, the struggling snail produces large quantities of slime which clogs up the snake's nasal openings; while extracting the snail, the snake relies, therefore, on air stored in its lungs to breathe.

COLUBRIDAE:
Colubrine Snake Family

The colubrine family is the largest of the three groups of advanced snakes and contains some 1,800 species — two-thirds of all living snakes. Although a convenient assemblage of species, this large and extremely diverse family may not be a natural one, and it is often divided into subfamilies in an attempt to clarify the relationships. Colubrids are found on all continents except Antarctica.

There is as much variation within the Colubrine family as there is between the other two families of advanced snakes, the Vipers and Elapids, but there are a few shared characteristics. No colubrids have any vestiges of a pelvis or hind limbs, and all have the left lung reduced or even absent (for streamlining of the body). The lower jaw is flexible, but there are no hollow poison-injecting fangs. Instead there are solid teeth on both jaws and, in some cases, teeth on the upper jaw, with grooves which are connected to a poison gland (rear-fanged snakes).

Most colubrids are harmless; all those which are dangerous, such as the boomslang (*Dispholidus typus*) and the twig snake (*Thelotornis kirtlandii*), occur in Africa.

Colubrids occur in all habitats, and there are ground-dwelling, arboreal, burrowing, even aquatic species. All are predators, feeding on anything from insects to small mammals. Most colubrids lay eggs, but some reproduce by giving birth to fully formed live young.

NAME: Spotted Water Snake, *Enhydris punctata*
RANGE: Australia: coast of Northern Territory
HABITAT: creeks, swamps, rivers
SIZE: 30–50 cm (11¾–19¾ in)

The spotted water snake is one of a subfamily of about 34 colubrids, all specialized for life in water. It is able to move on land as well as in water and comes ashore to bask on river banks and shores. Its small eyes are directed upward and its nostrils, too, are on the upper surface of the head. Pads of skin close off the nostrils completely when the snake is diving.

Mildly venomous, the water snake is rear-fanged — grooved teeth at the back of the upper jaw are connected to a poison gland. It preys on aquatic creatures such as fish and frogs. Females give birth to fully formed live young.

NAME: White-bellied Mangrove Snake, *Fordonia leucobalia*
RANGE: coast of N. Australia, S. E. Asia
HABITAT: mangroves
SIZE: 60 cm–1 m (23½ in–3¼ ft)

A member of the subfamily of aquatic colubrids, the white-bellied mangrove snake has similar adaptations to those of the rest of its group, such as nostrils near the top of its head and upward-facing eyes. Large numbers of these snakes frequent the edges of swamps, where they forage among the roots for food. It is a rear-fanged snake and feeds mainly on crabs, which seem strongly affected by its venom, unlike frogs and mammals, which are not. Fish are also included in its diet. If alarmed, the snake will take refuge in a crab burrow.

NAME: Egg-eating Snake, *Dasypeltis scabra*
RANGE: Africa, south and east of the Sahara
HABITAT: woodland, scrub
SIZE: 75 cm (29½ in)

This slender snake is one of the few snakes to exist entirely on hard-shelled birds' eggs. It hunts for eggs on the ground and in trees, mainly at night, although it is sometimes active during the day. Most other snakes take only the softer-shelled lizard and snake eggs, since they lack the specialized equipment that the snakes of this subfamily have for dealing with their hard, unwieldy prey.

The egg-eating snake's mouth and jaws are extremely flexible and are hinged in such a way as to accommodate large eggs. It has only a few small teeth in each jaw, but special projections of the neck vertebrae form a serrated edge of "teeth" which pierce the wall of the oesophagus.

When the snake swallows an egg, which may be twice the size of its head, it pushes its mouth against the egg, gradually engulfing it in its jaws, while stretching the elastic ligament joining the two halves of the lower jaw to the utmost. The small neck scales stand apart in rows, exposing the skin beneath. The oesophagus teeth slit the egg open and the contents pass into the stomach, while a specialized valve rejects the shell which is regurgitated. When eggs are plentiful, the snake stores up fat in its body on which it lives during those seasons when few eggs are available.

Females of this species lay 8 to 14 eggs, which they deposit singly and not in a clutch — an unusual habit for an egg-laying snake.

Fimbrios klossi

EGG-EATING SNAKE

SLUG SNAKE

SPOTTED WATER SNAKE

WHITE-BELLIED MANGROVE SNAKE

SNAIL-EATING SNAKE

Colubrine Snakes 2

NAME: **Grass Snake**, *Natrix natrix*
RANGE: **Europe: Scandinavia, south to Mediterranean countries; N. W. Africa; Asia, east to Lake Baikal, USSR**
HABITAT: **damp meadows, marshes, ditches, river banks**
SIZE: **up to 1.2 m (4 ft); occasionally up to 2 m (6½ ft)**

One of a group of colubrids adapted for life in water, the grass snake swims well and spends some time in water, although it is less aquatic than some other *Natrix* species. It is one of the most common and widespread European snakes, and 3 subspecies, which differ in coloration and pattern, occur over its large range. Females are generally longer and thicker-bodied than males.

The grass snake is active during the day, hunting for food in water and on land. It preys mainly on frogs, toads and newts but also takes fish and occasionally even small mammals and young birds. Much of its prey is swallowed alive, although it does have a venomous secretion that is toxic to small animals but harmless to man.

Depending on the latitude, grass snakes start to breed from April onward. The male courts the female, rubbing his chin, on which there are many sensory tubercles, over her body. If all goes well, he works his way up to her neck and they intertwine and mate. Some 8 or more weeks later, the female lays her 30 to 40 eggs, which are already fairly advanced in embryonic development. She deposits the eggs in a warm spot, preferably in decaying organic matter such as manure or compost heaps. The young hatch after 1 or 2 months, depending on the warmth of their surroundings.

NAME: **Dark-green Whip Snake**, *Coluber viridiflavus*
RANGE: **Europe: N.E. Spain, central and S. France, Italy, S. Switzerland, Yugoslavia, Corsica, Sardinia**
HABITAT: **dry, vegetated areas: hillsides, woodland edge, gardens**
SIZE: **up to 1.9 m (6¼ ft)**

A slender, elongate snake, the dark-green whip snake has a rounded snout, large eyes and a long tapering tail. Some individuals may, in fact, be almost all black, rather than dark green. Males are generally longer than females. Usually active in the daytime, it is a ground-dwelling snake but can climb well on rocks and bushes. It locates its prey by sight and usually feeds on lizards, frogs, mammals, birds and other snakes.

Males compete fiercely for mates in the breeding season. The female lays her 5 to 15 eggs among rocks or in cracks in the soil. The young hatch in 6 to 8 weeks.

NAME: **Bibron's Burrowing Viper**, *Atractaspis bibroni*
RANGE: **South Africa**
HABITAT: **dry, sandy regions**
SIZE: **up to 80 cm (31½ in)**

Also known as the southern mole viper, this snake is a member of a group of burrowing colubrids called mole vipers, all of which are found in Africa and the Middle East. Like its relatives, it has a shovel-shaped head, no distinct neck, a rounded, slender body and short tail. Its eyes are small.

A venomous snake, the mole viper has a sophisticated venom apparatus similar to that of the true vipers and, because of this, it was originally believed to be a viper. Its fangs are huge, relative to the small head, and can be folded or erected independently of each other. Once swung into the attack position, the fangs eject venom which is pumped into them from the connected poison glands.

The mole viper burrows into the soil with its strong snout, usually emerging at the surface only at night after rain. If on the surface in sunlight, it coils itself into a ball and hides its head in the coils. It feeds on other reptiles, such as burrowing lizards and blind snakes, which it kills with its venomous bite.

The female mole vipers reproduce by laying eggs.

NAME: **Red-bellied Snake**, *Storeria occipitomaculata*
RANGE: **extreme S. Canada; E. USA: Maine to Minnesota, south to Texas and Florida**
HABITAT: **woodland on hills and mountains, bogs**
SIZE: **20–40.5 cm (7¾–16 in)**

There are 3 subspecies of this widely distributed snake which vary in coloration and the arrangement of the characteristic bright spots on the neck; in the Florida subspecies the spots may be fused, forming a collar. The red-bellied snake lives from sea-level to 1,700 m (5,600 ft) and is active mostly at night, when it preys on insects and small invertebrates such as earthworms and slugs. If alarmed it can curl its upper lip in threat, while discharging a musky secretion from its cloacal opening.

The snakes mate in spring or autumn; before copulation, the male throws his body into a series of waves from tail to head and rubs his chin, equipped with sensory tubercles, over the female's body. He also has sensory tubercles around the cloaca (genital opening) region which appear to help him position himself correctly. The young develop inside the female's body and are born fully formed and measuring 7 to 10 cm (2¾ to 4 in).

NAME: **Common Garter Snake**, *Thamnophis sirtalis*
RANGE: **S. Canada; USA, except desert regions**
HABITAT: **damp country, often near water: marshes, meadows, ditches, farmland, woodland**
SIZE: **45 cm–1.3 m (17¾ in–4¼ ft)**

The most widely distributed snake in North America and one of the most familiar, the garter snake occurs in many subspecies over its huge range. The coloration is, therefore, extremely variable, but the garter snake nearly always has distinctive back and side stripes. It is active during the day and hunts for frogs, toads, salamanders and small invertebrates among damp vegetation on the ground. One of the few snakes to occur in the far north, the garter snake withstands cold weather well and is found as far as 67° North. In the south of its range, it may remain active all year round, but in the north it hibernates in communal dens.

Garter snakes usually mate in spring, sometimes communally as they emerge from hibernation. They may, however, mate in autumn, in which event the sperm spend most of the winter in the female's oviduct and do not move into position to fertilize the eggs until spring. Before copulation, the male snake throws his body into a series of waves and then rubs his chin over the female's body. The tubercles on his chin must receive the right sensory responses before he will mate. As many as 80 young develop inside the female's body, nourished by a form of placenta, and are born fully formed.

NAME: **Rat Snake**, *Elaphe obsoleta*
RANGE: **S. Canada; USA: Vermont to Minnesota, south to Texas and Florida; N. Mexico**
HABITAT: **forest, swamps, farmland, wooded slopes**
SIZE: **86 cm–2.5 m (33¾ in–8¼ ft)**

A large, powerful species, the rat snake tolerates a variety of habitats in wet and dry situations. There are 6 or more subspecies which occur in one of three main colour patterns: plain, blotched or striped. It is an agile snake, good at climbing, and hunts rodents and other small mammals, birds and lizards in trees and in barns or ruined buildings. Usually active during the day, it may tend to be nocturnal in summer. In much of its range, it hibernates throughout the winter.

Rat snakes mate in spring and autumn. The female lays 5 to 30 eggs in leaf debris or under a rock or log. The eggs hatch in 2 to 4 months, depending on the temperature: the warmer the weather, the quicker they hatch.

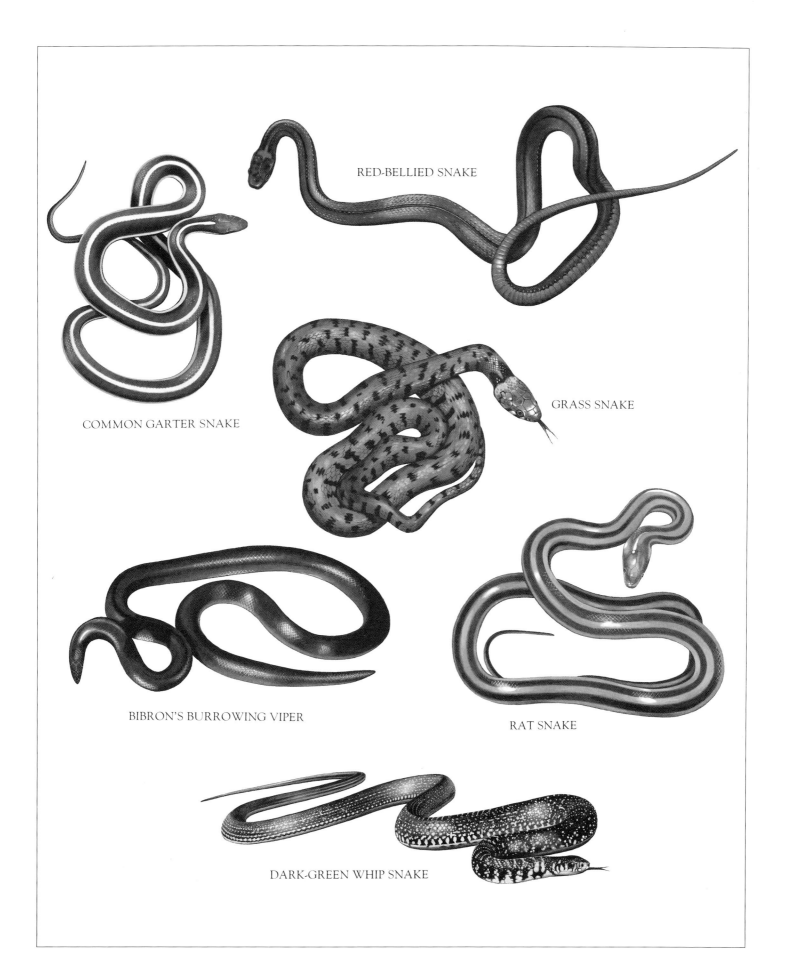

RED-BELLIED SNAKE

COMMON GARTER SNAKE

GRASS SNAKE

BIBRON'S BURROWING VIPER

RAT SNAKE

DARK-GREEN WHIP SNAKE

Colubrine Snakes 3

NAME: **Smooth Snake,** *Coronella austriaca*
RANGE: **Europe: S. Scandinavia, S. England, south to N. Spain, Italy and Greece; east to USSR, N. Iran**
HABITAT: **dry rocky areas, heathland, open woodland**
SIZE: **50–80 cm (19¾–31½ in)**

The slender, round-bodied smooth snake varies in coloration over its wide range but nearly always has a dark streak on each side of its head. The head is fairly small and pointed and there is no clear neck. It is a secretive snake, although active in the daytime, and adapts to a variety of dry habitats up 1,800 m (5,900 ft); it is even occasionally found in moist areas. Although it rarely basks in full sun, the smooth snake likes to retreat to warm, shady areas under rocks or stones. Lizards, particularly lacertids, make up the bulk of its diet and it also eats small snakes, young mammals and insects. It holds its prey in a few coils of its body to subdue it while it starts to swallow.

In the breeding season, males fight one another for mates. The female gives birth to 2 to 15 live young in autumn; they emerge in transparent, membranous shells from which they free themselves immediately. The newly born young measure 12 to 20 cm (4¾ to 7¾ in) in length. Males mature at 3 years and females at 4.

NAME: **Common Kingsnake,** *Lampropeltis getulus*
RANGE: **USA: New Jersey to Florida in east, Oregon to California in west; Mexico**
HABITAT: **varied, forest, woodland, desert, prairie, swamps, marshes**
SIZE: **90 cm–2 m (35½ in–6½ ft)**

A large snake with smooth, shiny scales, the common kingsnake usually has alternating dark and light rings, but some of the many subspecies have more irregular speckled patterns. It is primarily a ground-dwelling species, although it may sometimes climb into small trees or bushes, and is active in the daytime, usually in the early morning and at dusk. Found in almost every type of habitat, it will take refuge under rocks, in vegetation and under logs. It feeds on snakes, including rattlesnakes and coral snakes, lizards, mice and birds which it kills by constriction, holding the prey in the powerful coils of its body until it suffocates. Indeed, the description "king" seems to be applied only to those snakes which feed on other snakes.

Kingsnakes mate in spring. The female lays 3 to 24 eggs which usually hatch in 2 to 3 months, depending on the warmth of the weather.

NAME: **Gopher Snake,** *Pituophis melanoleucas*
RANGE: **S. W. Canada; USA: west and central states, Florida; Mexico**
HABITAT: **dry woodland, grassland, prairies, rocky desert**
SIZE: **1.2–2.5 m (4–8¼ ft)**

The large, robust gopher snake is found in a variety of habitats and is a good climber and burrower. Its head is small and somewhat pointed and, although the coloration varies in the many subspecies over its wide range, most gopher snakes have pale bodies with black, brown or reddish markings.

Usually active by day, the gopher snake may become nocturnal in hot weather. It feeds largely on rodents, as well as on rabbits, birds and lizards, all of which it kills by constriction — throwing its powerful body coils around the victim until it suffocates. It may burrow underground for shelter or take over mammal or tortoise burrows. If alarmed, the gopher snake flattens its head, hisses loudly and vibrates its tail before attacking the enemy.

Gopher snakes mate in spring and the female lays up to 24 eggs in a burrow or beneath a rock or log. The young hatch in 9 to 11 weeks and are up to 45 cm (17¾ in) long on hatching.

NAME: **Paradise Tree Snake,** *Chrysopelea paradisi*
RANGE: **S.E. Asia: Philippines to Indonesia**
HABITAT: **forest**
SIZE: **up to 1.2 m (4 ft)**

Also known as the flying snake, this species does in fact glide from tree to tree, from one branch down to another. It launches itself into the air, its body stretched out and its belly pulled in to make a concave surface with maximum resistance to the air. In this position it glides downward at an angle of 50 or 60 degrees to the ground for 20 m (65 ft) or more and lands safely without injuring itself. It seems to have little control over its "flight", however, and cannot glide upward or steer with any degree of efficiency.

A further adaptation for its tree-dwelling life are the ridged scales on the snake's belly which help it to climb almost vertically up tree trunks. The ridges are thrust against the bark and enable the snake to gain a hold on every tiny irregularity of surface. Thus, it can ascend right into the trees, where few other snakes can go, and feed on the abundant tree-dwelling lizards. The closely related oriental tree snake, C. ornata, can glide and climb in the same manner.

The female paradise tree snake lays up to 12 eggs.

NAME: **Mangrove Snake,** *Boiga dendrophila*
RANGE: **S. E. Asia: Philippines to Indonesia**
HABITAT: **forest, mangroves**
SIZE: **2.5 m (8¼ ft)**

The beautifully marked mangrove snake has a slender body with hexagonal scales on its back and sides. Primarily an arboreal species, it hunts birds in the trees but may also descend to the ground to prey on rodents. It is a venomous, rear-fanged snake: the grooved teeth toward the back of the jaw carry venom from the poison gland above the jaw into the prey.

The female mangrove snake lays 4 to 7 eggs.

NAME: **Boomslang,** *Dispholidus typus*
RANGE: **Africa: central to South Africa**
HABITAT: **savanna**
SIZE: **up to 2 m (6½ ft)**

The boomslang is one of only two dangerously poisonous snakes in the colubrid family. It has three large grooved fangs, set farther forward than the usual two fangs of colubrids, and extremely toxic venom which causes respiratory failure and haemorrhaging and can even kill a human being. Normally, however, it uses its venomous bites on lizards, particularly chameleons, and on frogs and birds.

The boomslang is a tree-dwelling snake, usually active in the daytime. It varies in coloration but is usually predominantly black, brown or green on the upper surface.

The female boomslang lays 10 to 14 eggs.

NAME: **Vine Snake,** *Oxybelis fulgidus*
RANGE: **Central America to N. South America**
HABITAT: **rain forest, cultivated land**
SIZE: **1.5–2 m (5–6½ ft)**

Barely the thickness of a man's finger, about 1.25 cm (½ in) in diameter at the most, the vine snake is a remarkably slender, elongate species. As it lies amid the branches of forest trees, its proportions and greeny-brown coloration make it almost indistinguishable from the abundant creepers and vines. Its head, too, is thin and elongate and equipped with rear fangs and mild venom.

A slow-moving predator, active in the daytime and at night, the vine snake feeds mainly on young birds which it steals from nests and on lizards. If threatened, it puffs up the front of its body, revealing vivid coloration usually hidden under scales, and opens its long mouth wide. A frightened snake may also sway from side to side, like a stem in the breeze.

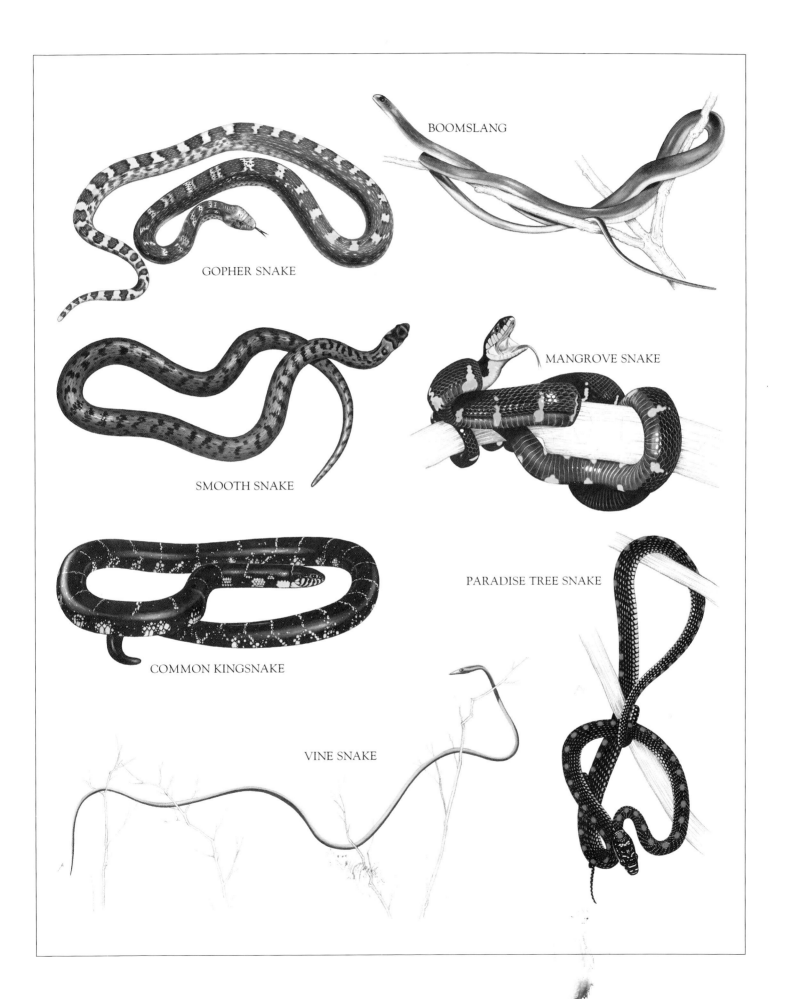

BOOMSLANG

GOPHER SNAKE

MANGROVE SNAKE

SMOOTH SNAKE

PARADISE TREE SNAKE

COMMON KINGSNAKE

VINE SNAKE

Cobras and Sea Snakes

NAME: Eastern Green Mamba,
Dendroaspis angusticeps
RANGE: E. and S. Africa
HABITAT: savanna
SIZE: 2 m (6½ ft)

The slender, fast-moving mambas spend much of their lives in trees, where they feed on birds and lizards. Their venom is extremely toxic, but these snakes are not generally aggressive unless provoked and tend rather to flee from danger or threat.

In the breeding season, two or three males compete in ritualized fights for females. They wrap their bodies around one another and threaten with their raised heads. Mating may last for many hours. The female lays her 10 to 15 eggs in a hole in the ground or in a hollow tree stump. The young mambas hatch in 17 to 18 weeks.

NAME: De Vis's Banded Snake, *Denisonia devisii*
**RANGE: Australia: N. New South Wales,
S. Queensland**
HABITAT: dry, wooded areas
SIZE: 50 cm (19¾ in)

A nocturnal species, this snake shelters under leaf litter or a log during the day and emerges at night to hunt for food, mainly lizards, which it kills with its toxic venom. It has a distinctive defence posture which it often adopts when threatened: it flattens its body, which is thrown into a series of stiff curves, and then lashes out and bites if approached.

The female gives birth to about 8 live young, which have developed inside her body, nourished by a form of placenta.

NAME: King Cobra, *Ophiophagus hannah*
**RANGE: India, S. China, Malaysia to
Philippines and Indonesia**
HABITAT: forest, often near water
SIZE: 4–5.5 m (13–18 ft)

The biggest poisonous snake in the world, the king cobra's head can be as big as a man's. It can make itself still more impressive by adopting the cobra threat posture, with the flexible neck ribs and loose skin spread out to form a wide hood. Despite its size, it is an agile, secretive snake and will flee into cover or even water if pursued. It feeds mainly on other snakes — its scientific name means "snake-eater" — but also on monitor lizards.

The female king cobra constructs a nest of vegetation for her eggs, perhaps the only snake to do so. She gathers together twigs, branches and foliage with a coil of her forebody and then makes a chamber in the middle of them by revolving her coiled body. She lays her 18 to 40 eggs in this chamber, covers them and lies coiled on top of the nest while they incubate.

ELAPIDAE:
Cobra and Sea Snake Family

There are about 250 species of highly venomous snake in this family, found mainly in tropical and subtropical areas of Australia, Asia, Africa (except Madagascar) and America. Elapids are most abundant in Australia.

The family is often divided into two groups: the elapids proper, including cobras, kraits, mambas and coral snakes, all of which are land- or tree-dwelling; and the sea snakes. The 50 of so species of sea snake lead entirely aquatic lives; most are marine but a few live in lakes or enter rivers. All elapids have fangs, situated near the front of the upper jaw, which are either deeply grooved for the transport of venom or have grooves the edges of which have fused to form a venom canal.

NAME: Indian Cobra, *Naja naja*
RANGE: India, central Asia, S.E. Asia
**HABITAT: rain forest, rice fields,
cultivated land**
SIZE: 1.8–2.2 m (6–7¼ ft)

A large, highly venomous snake, the Indian cobra feeds on rodents, lizards and frogs. As well as biting, the Indian cobra can attack or defend itself from a distance by "spitting" venom which, if it enters the opponent's eyes, causes severe pain and damage. The snake actually forces the venom through its fangs, by exerting muscular pressure on the venom glands, so that it sprays out in twin jets for 2 m (6½ ft) or more.

In its characteristic threat posture, the Indian cobra raises the front one-third of its body and spreads out its long flexible neck ribs and loose skin to form a disclike hood, which has markings resembling eyes on the back.

Indian cobras pay more attention to their eggs than is usual in snakes. The 8 to 45 eggs (usually 12 to 20) are laid in a hollow tree, a termite mound or earth into which the snakes tunnel. The female guards the clutch throughout the incubation period, leaving them only for a short time each day to feed. The young hatch after about 50 or 60 days.

NAME: Eastern Brown Snake, *Pseudonaja textilis*
RANGE: E. Australia, E. New Guinea
HABITAT: wet forest, rocky hillsides
SIZE: 1.5 m (5 ft)

A fast-moving, venomous snake, this species is equally at home in dry or swampy land. It is active during the day and feeds on small mammals, frogs and lizards. Its coloration varies from yellow to dark brown with bands of varying intensity.

NAME: Bandy-bandy, *Vermicella annulata*
**RANGE: Australia (not extreme S.E.,
S.W. or N.W.)**
**HABITAT: varied, damp forest to desert
sandhills**
SIZE: 40 cm (15¾ in)

A distinctive black and white snake, the rings of the bandy-bandy vary in width and number, between males and females and geographically. It is a nocturnal snake and feeds mainly, if not exclusively, on blind snakes (Typhlopidae). Although venomous, its fangs and venom supply are too small to cause harm to anything other than small animals.

An egg-laying species, the female deposits her eggs under rocks or logs.

NAME: Eastern Coral Snake, *Micrurus fulvius*
**RANGE: USA: North Carolina to Florida,
west to Texas; Mexico**
**HABITAT: forest, often near water, rocky
hillsides**
SIZE: 56 cm–1.2 m (22 in–4 ft)

One of the only two elapids in North America, the Eastern coral snake is a colourful species, with red, black and yellow or white bands ringing its body. The bright markings of these poisonous snakes may serve to warn off potential predators. The coral snake is a secretive species, spending much of the time buried in leaf litter or sand. In the morning and late afternoon, it prowls on the surface in search of small lizards and snakes, which it kills with its highly toxic venom.

The female lays 3 to 12 eggs which hatch in about 3 months.

NAME: Banded Sea Snake, *Hydrophis cyanocinctus*
**RANGE: Persian Gulf, Indian Ocean,
Pacific Ocean to Japan**
HABITAT: coastal waters
SIZE: 2 m (6½ ft)

The banded sea snake is fully adapted to aquatic life and never goes on land. Its body is laterally flattened and its tail is paddle-shaped for propulsion when swimming. It does breathe air but can remain submerged for up to 2 hours. Its nostrils are directed upward and can be closed off by pads of tissue bordering the front of the nostrils. The snake's body muscles have degenerated and, if washed ashore, it collapses helplessly. Like all sea snakes, this species feeds on fish and has extremely toxic venom. The venom of one sea snake, *Enhydrina schistosa*, has been shown in laboratory tests to be more powerful than that of any other snake.

All but one sea snake bear live young in the water. The banded sea snake gives birth to 2 to 6 young.

EASTERN CORAL SNAKE

BANDED SEA SNAKE

DE VIS'S BANDED SNAKE

KING COBRA

INDIAN COBRA

EASTERN BROWN SNAKE

BANDY-BANDY

EASTERN GREEN MAMBA

Vipers

NAME: **Common Viper** *Vipera berus*
RANGE: **Britain, Europe to Siberia**
HABITAT: **moors, meadows, chalk hills, forest edge**
SIZE: **up to 50 cm (19¾ in)**

The widely distributed common viper, or adder, is active in the daytime in the north of its range where it takes every opportunity to bask in the sun. Farther south, it is active in the evening and at night. In winter it must hibernate, often using the abandoned burrow of another creature, until the temperature rises to an average of about 8°C (46°F) — the length of hibernation, therefore, varies with latitude. This viper moves slowly and does not climb but is a good swimmer. Mice, voles, shrews, lizards and frogs, all of which it kills with its venom, are its main foods, and it may occasionally take birds' eggs.

In the mating season, which may occur only every other year in areas where the hibernation period is long, males perform ritualistic aggressive dances before mating. They rear up in front of one another, swaying and trying to push each other over. The female retains her 3 to 20 eggs in the body until they are on the point of hatching. The young are about 18 cm (7 in) long when they hatch and are already equipped with venom and fangs.

NAME: **Desert Sidewinding Viper,** *Vipera peringuey*
RANGE: **Africa: Namibia**
HABITAT: **desert**
SIZE: **25.5 cm (10 in)**

A small, rare viper, this species is found on the coastal sand-dunes of the Namib desert. It glides over the dunes with a sidewinding motion of lateral waves, leaving tracks like two parallel grooves where two parts of the body touch the sand and support the snake. During the day it half-buries itself in the sand — a feat it can accomplish in about 20 seconds — to shelter from the sun or to lie in wait for prey such as rodents or lizards.

NAME: **Horned Viper,** *Vipera ammodytes*
RANGE: **Europe: Austria, Hungary, Balkan peninsula**
HABITAT: **arid, sandy regions**
SIZE: **76 cm (30 in)**

Identifiable by the small horn on its snout, this viper is also called the sand viper because of its preference for sandy areas. Like many European vipers, it avoids woodland but is found in clearings, paths and often in vineyards. Its movements generally are slow, but it can strike rapidly with its fangs to kill small mammals, lizards, snakes and small birds. Horned vipers hibernate throughout the winter.

VIPERIDAE: Viper Family

There are 40 species of viper, found all over the Old World except in Australia and Madagascar. Most species are short, sturdy snakes which live on the ground; a few species have become arboreal and have prehensile tails.

Vipers do not chase their prey — lizards, small mammals and birds — but wait in a concealed position to ambush and strike. They have a sophisticated fang and venom system: the large hollow fangs, which fold back when the mouth is closed, swing forward and become erect when the mouth is opened wide. Venom is pumped into them from venom glands at the base of the fangs and, as they pierce the victim, the poison is injected.

NAME: **Gaboon Viper,** *Vipera gabonica*
RANGE: **W. Africa, south of the Sahara to South Africa**
HABITAT: **rain forest**
SIZE: **1.2–2 m (4–6½ ft)**

One of the largest vipers, the Gaboon viper is well camouflaged, as it lies among the leaf litter on the forest floor, by the complex geometric patterns on its skin. It has a broad head, slender neck and stout body, tapering to a thin tail. Its fangs, the longest of any viper, are up to 5 cm (2 in) long and are supplied with a venom which causes haemorrhaging in the victim and inhibits breathing and heartbeat.

The Gaboon viper is nocturnal and, although it moves little, manages to find plenty of prey, such as rodents, frogs, toads and ground-living birds, on the forest floor. The female bears live young in litters of up to 30 at a time; each young snake is about 30.5 cm (12 in) long at birth.

NAME: **Aspic Viper** *Vipera aspis*
RANGE: **Europe: France, Germany, Switzerland, Italy, Sicily**
HABITAT: **warm dry areas up to 3,000 m (9,800 ft)**
SIZE: **up to 76 cm (30 in)**

Also known as the European asp, this species varies in coloration from area to area. A sluggish snake except when alarmed, it spends much of its time basking in the sun on a tree stump or rock, particularly in the early morning or late afternoon. It feeds on small mammals, lizards and nestling birds.

Mating takes place in the spring, after males have performed ritualistic combat displays, and females lay 4 to 18 eggs. In winter, aspic vipers hibernate singly or in groups in underground burrows or in wall crevices.

NAME: **Puff Adder,** *Bitis arietans*
RANGE: **Africa: Morocco, south of the Sahara to South Africa; Middle East**
HABITAT: **savanna up to 1,800 m (6,000 ft)**
SIZE: **1.4–2 m (4½–6½ ft)**

Perhaps the most common and widespread African snake, the puff adder adapts to both moist and arid climates but not to the extremes of desert or rain forest. It is one of the biggest vipers, with a girth of up to 23 cm (9 in), and can inflate its body to an even larger size when about to strike. Its fangs are about 1.25 cm (½ in) long, and the venom causes haemorrhaging in the victim.

Primarily a ground-living snake, the sluggish puff adder relies on its cryptic pattern and coloration to conceal it from both enemies and potential prey. It occasionally climbs into trees and is a good swimmer. Ground-living mammals, such as rats and mice, and birds, lizards, frogs and toads are its main prey.

The female puff adder lays 20 to 40 eggs which develop inside her body and hatch minutes after laying. The young are 15 to 20 cm (6 to 7¾ in) long when they hatch and can kill small mice.

NAME: **Saw-scaled Adder,** *Echis carinatus*
RANGE: **N. Africa to Syria, Iran, east to India**
HABITAT: **arid, sandy regions**
SIZE: **53–72 cm (20¾–28¼ in)**

An extremely dangerous snake, the saw-scaled adder is responsible for the majority of human deaths from snake bite in North Africa. This adder uses some serrated scales on its sides to make a threatening noise: it coils its body into a tight spiral and then moves the coils so that the scales rub against one another, making a loud rasping sound. It is these scales which give the snake its common name.

The saw-scaled adder often uses a sideways motion, known as sidewinding, when on sandy ground. It throws its body, only two short sections of which touch the ground, into lateral waves. All the adder's weight is, therefore, pushing against the ground at these points, so providing the leverage to push it sideways.

During the day, the saw-scaled adder lies sheltered from the heat under a fallen tree trunk or rock, or flattens its body and digs into the sand by means of the "keeled" lateral scales. It feeds at night on small rodents, skinks, geckos, frogs and large invertebrates such as centipedes and scorpions. Breeding usually takes place in the rainy season, and the female lays about 5 eggs. The young adders are about 20 cm (7¾ in) long when they hatch.

SAW-SCALED ADDER

GABOON VIPER

ASPIC VIPER

HORNED VIPER

COMMON VIPER

PUFF ADDER

DESERT SIDEWINDING VIPER

Pit Vipers

NAME: **Massasauga**, *Sistrurus catenatus*
RANGE: **USA: N. W. Pennsylvania to Arizona; N. Mexico**
HABITAT: **varied, swamp, marshland, woodland, prairie**
SIZE: **45 cm–1m (17¾ in–3¼ ft)**

The massasauga tolerates a wide range of habitat and, although it seems to prefer swampy land, occurs even in arid grassland in the west of its range. It has up to eight rattles on its tail and is distinguished from other rattlers by the nine enlarged scales on its head. It preys on lizards, frogs, insects, small mammals and birds.

In April or May, the massasaugas mate and a litter of 2 to 19 live young is born in the summer.

NAME: **Sidewinder**, *Crotalus cerastes*
RANGE: **S. W. USA: S. California, Nevada and Utah, south to Mexico**
HABITAT: **desert, rocky hillsides**
SIZE: **43–82 cm (17–32¼ in)**

A small agile snake, the sidewinder has a distinctive hornlike projection over each eye. It is chiefly nocturnal and takes refuge in the burrow of another animal or under a bush during the day. At night it emerges to hunt its prey, mainly small rodents, such as pocket mice and kangaroo rats, and lizards. A desert inhabitant, this snake moves with a sideways motion, known as sidewinding, thought to be the most efficient mode of movement for a snake on sand. It throws its body into lateral waves, only two short sections of it touching the ground. All the snake's weight, therefore, is pushing against the ground at these points, and this provides the leverage to move it sideways. As it travels, the snake leaves a trail of parallel J-shaped markings. An ideal form of movement in open, sparsely vegetated country, sidewinding has the advantage of reducing contact between the snake's body and the hot sand.

Sidewinders mate in April or May, and the female gives birth to 5 to 18 live young about 3 months later.

NAME: **Fer-de-Lance**, *Bothrops atrox*
RANGE: **S. Mexico to South America; West Indies**
HABITAT: **low coastal areas**
SIZE: **2.45 m (8 ft)**

A common pit viper, the fer-de-lance varies in colour and pattern over its wide range. A sheath of membranous flesh covers its fangs, but when the snake bites, the sheath is pushed back. The fer-de-lance feeds mainly on small mammals, and its venom causes rapid and severe internal bleeding. The female is an unusually prolific breeder for a pit viper, giving birth to up to 50 live young in a yearly litter.

CROTALIDAE: Pit Viper Family

The pit vipers are a group of highly venomous snakes. They occur in eastern Europe and throughout mainland Asia and Japan, but the group is best known for its New World representatives such as rattlesnakes. Pit vipers are closely related to true vipers (Viperidae) and are considered by some experts to be a subfamily of Viperidae. There are about 123 species. Unlike the true vipers, pit vipers are absent from Africa and they possess some significant anatomical differences.

The most important of these differences are the organs which give the snakes their common name: sensory pits on each side of the head in front of and just below the eyes. These pits can detect heat and are used by these nocturnal snakes to locate warm-blooded prey, the body-temperature of which is higher than the surroundings. A pit viper can discern and strike accurately at prey by moving its head from side to side and using both pit organs to discover the distance and direction of the animal. Once it has located its prey, the pit viper kills by a rapid strike, in which the long, curved fangs of the upper jaw impale the target and inject venom. Small or weak creatures may be swallowed whole without poisoning, but larger, more active prey must first be subdued with venom.

One group of pit vipers, the rattlesnakes, have characteristic tail rattles. The rattle is a series of flattened, interlocking hollow segments on the tail which make a noise when the tail is shaken. Each of these segments was once the tip of the tail, and a new one is added each time the snake sheds its skin. However, earlier rattles fall off, and there are rarely more than 14 rattles at any time. The sound produced is used to warn potential enemies to keep their distance.

NAME: **Eastern Diamondback Rattlesnake**, *Crotalus adamanteus*
RANGE: **E. USA: North Carolina to Florida Keys, west to Louisiana**
HABITAT: **woodland, farmland**
SIZE: **91 cm–2.4 m (35¾ in–7¾ ft)**

The largest rattler, the eastern diamondback is the most dangerous snake in North America, with venom that attacks the blood tissue. Its striking diamond-patterned skin provides camouflage as it lies coiled in vegetation, watching for prey such as rabbits and birds.

The female diamondback bears 8 to 12 live young, each measuring 30 to 36 cm (11¾ to 14¼ in), in late summer and defends them aggressively.

NAME: **Cottonmouth**, *Agkistrodon piscivorus*
RANGE: **S. and S. E. USA**
HABITAT: **marshes, streams, lakes, swamps**
SIZE: **51 cm–1.9 m (20 in–6¼ ft)**

The heavy-bodied cottonmouth spends much of its life in or near water and swims well, holding its head up out of the water. It is most active at night, when it preys on amphibians, fish, snakes and birds, and it is one of the few snakes to eat carrion. An extremely dangerous species, its venom is haemotoxic — it destroys the red blood cells and coagulates the blood around the bite. The venom is actually extracted and used medically for its coagulating properties in the treatment of haemorrhagic conditions.

Female cottonmouths breed every other year and produce litters of up to 15 young which measure 18 to 33 cm (7 to 13 in) at birth.

NAME: **Manushi/Asiatic Pit Viper**, *Agkistrodon halys*
RANGE: **Caspian Sea area, S. USSR, China**
HABITAT: **steppe, semi-desert, taiga (coniferous forest)**
SIZE: **46–76 cm (18–30 in)**

One of the few pit vipers in the Old World, the manushi is found as far as 51° North. Mainly nocturnal, it emerges at sunset to hunt its prey, which consists mostly of small mammals. Its venom is fatal to small creatures such as mice, but is seldom dangerous to larger animals and causes only mild temporary paralysis in man.

The manushi hibernates through the winter, awaking in March; males usually wake a week or more before females. Mating takes place shortly after the end of hibernation and the female lays 3 to 10 eggs which hatch about 3 months later.

NAME: **Bushmaster**, *Lachesis muta*
RANGE: **S. Nicaragua to Amazon basin of South America**
HABITAT: **rain forest**
SIZE: **2.45–3.5 m (8–11½ ft)**

A rare, deadly and formidable pit viper, the bushmaster is the largest of its family. It is strictly nocturnal, hiding during the day in a cave or tree hollow and emerging at night to hunt. It preys on small rodents and other mammals up to the size of small deer. Although its venom is not as poisonous as that of some pit vipers, the bushmaster produces such large quantities of poison, and has such huge fangs with which to inject it, that it is one of the world's most dangerous snakes. The female bushmaster is the only New World viper to lay eggs.

SIDEWINDER

MANUSHI

COTTONMOUTH

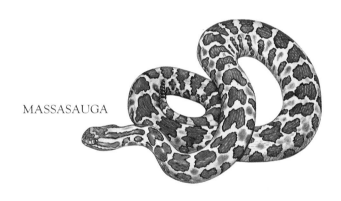

MASSASAUGA

EASTERN DIAMONDBACK RATTLESNAKE

BUSHMASTER

FER-DE-LANCE

Amphibians – the first land vertebrates

Compared with the huge numbers of existing fishes, reptiles, birds and mammals, the total global count of living amphibian species is rather meagre. Only about 2,000 forms, divided into about 250 genera, are authoritatively recognized at present.

All modern forms can be accommodated in three major sub-groupings, of which two are commonly recognizable animal types: first, the Urodela (newts and salamanders), and second, the Anura (frogs and toads). The third group is the Apoda, which contains several families of limbless, elongate burrowing amphibians known as caecilians.

The amphibians were the first group of vertebrates to colonize the land. The distant evolutionary origins of amphibianlike animals from fish ancestors are a key phase in vertebrate evolution, heralding as they do all the subsequent developments of land-living vertebrates. Probably between 375 and 350 million years ago, lobed fin fishes (crossopterygians), which already possessed lungs and four solidly constructed, downward-directed fins, began, more and more, to move out of freshwater habitats into adjacent terrestrial ones. The development of amphibians had begun.

Almost all the early amphibians must have retained fishlike habits. They were entirely or largely aquatic and were fish-eating animals like their crossopterygian ancestors. (The only known living relative of the crossopterygian fishes is the coelacanth.) Only a few of these early amphibians were truly terrestrial forms.

Of the modern amphibians, it is the newts and salamanders that have kept the most fishlike appearance, with elongate bodies, sinuous swimming movements in water and dorsal and ventral fins on the body. Larval and adult newts and salamanders are relatively similar to one another in these respects, and adults frequently possess some larval characteristics.

The anuran frogs and toads all have a characteristic shortened body with no true tail. This dramatic alteration of the primitive, long-bodied amphibian has opened up a wide range of opportunities for new ways of living. In general, the limbs have become more powerful. Jumping and climbing have been developed to a considerable degree in many species and others have become efficient burrowers. The caecilians (order Apoda) are extraordinary earthwormlike amphibians which are highly adapted for a burrowing life: the skull of the caecilian is solid and bony, the limbs have completely disappeared.

Amphibians as a group demonstrate an interesting range of methods of locomotion, some very fishlike, others more suitable for life on land. Newts and salamanders have two basic forms of movement on land: when in haste, they move much as they do in water, by a sinuous wriggling of the body with little motion of the limbs; when moving more slowly, the body is lifted off the ground and supported on the four limbs, which move in the typical manner of four-legged vertebrates.

Frogs and toads, having lost their swimming tail, possess a completely different means of progression. Double, synchronized kicks of the long back legs are used for swimming in water and hopping and jumping on land. Both frogs and toads can also walk. Several groups of frogs and toads have independently developed rather similar specializations for moving in trees: they have adhesive pads on elongate toes enabling them to climb in vegetation. The limbless caecilians move by sinuous undulations similar to those of snakes.

Just as locomotion in amphibians is a fascinating amalgam of fishlike and terrestrial attributes, respiration shows a similar intriguing mix of "technologies". Amphibians may possess gills which are externally visible or tucked away inside a flap of skin. In both instances, the gills are developed from the outer skin and are not equivalent to the more internally placed gills of fishes. The gills are used by larval or adult amphibians for gaseous exchange (oxygen in, carbon dioxide out) in water. Amphibians on land use a mixture of two different mechanisms for the same function. Most possess lungs — paired sacs which open ultimately into the mouth cavity. This buccal cavity is used as a pump chamber to pull air in through the nostrils, before pushing it alternately a few times between lungs and mouth, then expelling it through the nostrils. The skin of the buccal cavity is itself well supplied with blood vessels and acts as a minor extension of the respiratory surface of the lungs.

In a similar way, the moist scaleless skin of the amphibians is also important for gaseous exchange. Indeed, the vital need of amphibians to keep their bodies moist for respiration is a major constraint on their utilization of habitats. Only rarely are they able to be active in potentially drying conditions. It also limits their size because, as an animal increases in size, its surface area becomes smaller in proportion to its body volume. A large amphibian, therefore, has a correspondingly less adequate area of respiratory skin to provide for its larger body.

Like the reptiles, amphibians operate on a quite different basis of energy balance from that of birds and mammals. The latter two groups maintain a constant high temperature, somewhere between 36°C and 42°C (96.8°F and 107.6°F). Amphibians and reptiles, on the other hand, have body temperatures close to that of the air or water in which they live and gain heat by basking in the sun. They are dependent on external temperature or sunlight for full activity. They can, however, exist on smaller amounts of food than birds and mammals because of the low energy requirements of the cold-blooded condition.

Although two species of newt are known to be parthenogenetic (capable of virgin birth), all other amphibian species include both male and female forms. The females either lay eggs or produce live young. Almost all amphibians must return to water to breed, even those which are otherwise highly adapted to terrestrial conditions. A few species have sidestepped this constraint in extraordinary ways: for example, by providing a sac on the back in which egg development occurs.

In many amphibians, males and females have different appearances. In many frogs and toads, the males move to the water before the females and attract the latter with loud, species-specific calls. Males cling to the backs of the females, when mating, by means of roughened pads which develop on the hands, and fertilize the eggs externally as they are expelled. Newts have complex courtship rituals. The males expel their sperm in packets, called spermatophores, which the females pick up in their genital openings (cloacas); the sperm then fertilizes the eggs internally.

Most amphibians pass through a distinctive tadpole larval stage or series of stages, after the hatching of the jelly-covered eggs. During this tadpole phase, the larvae are fully aquatic and possess prominent fins; they progressively acquire adult characteristics such as limbs and lungs. In some species of tailed amphibians, sexual maturity is reached at a stage which in other species would be regarded as larval. This process of neoteny or paedogenesis (breeding as a larva) is partly connected with the effects of the hormone thyroxine, which is involved in larva-adult metamorphosis.

Although less adaptable and complex than the reptiles, birds and mammals, the amphibians in appropriate habitat conditions are clearly able to hold their own against other vertebrates. Due to their extremely low nutrient requirements, they are successful in conditions where food is sparse, seasonal or intermittent in availability.

Salamanders

ORDER URODELA

There are 8 families of salamanders, newts and allies in this order. All have elongate bodies and long tails.

CRYPTOBRANCHIDAE: Giant Salamander Family

This family contains the largest amphibians alive in the world today. Only 3 species are known: the Chinese and Japanese giant salamanders and the hellbender of the eastern USA. The Asiatic giant salamanders can reach lengths of over 1.5 m (5 ft).

NAME: **Hellbender,** *Cryptobranchus alleganiensis*
RANGE: **E. USA: S. New York to N. Alabama, Missouri**
HABITAT: **rocky-bottomed streams**
SIZE: **30.5–74 cm (12–29 in)**

Despite the implications of its common name, this giant salamander is a harmless creature which feeds on crayfish, snails and worms. It has the flattened head characteristic of its family and loose flaps of skin along the lower sides of its body.

A nocturnal salamander, the hellbender hides under rocks in the water during the day. It depends on its senses of smell and touch, rather than on sight, to find its prey, since its eyes are set so far down the sides of its head that it cannot focus on an object with both eyes at once.

Hellbenders breed in autumn: the male makes a hollow beneath a rock or log on the stream bed and the female lays strings of 200 to 500 eggs. As she lays the eggs, the male fertilizes them and then guards the nest until the eggs hatch 2 or 3 months later.

HYNOBIIDAE: Asiatic Land Salamander Family

The 30 species in this family are considered the most primitive of living salamanders. All occur in central and eastern Asia.

NAME: **Asian Salamander,** *Hynobius stejnegeri*
RANGE: **Japan**
HABITAT: **mountain streams**
SIZE: **14 cm (5½ in)**

Like all members of its family, the Asian salamander's methods of breeding are primitive, involving external fertilization. The female lays her eggs in water in paired sacs, each sac containing 35 to 70 eggs. The male then takes the sacs and fertilizes the eggs but shows no interest in the female.

SALAMANDRIDAE: Newt Family

There are about 42 species of salamander and newt in this family, found in temperate regions of northwest Africa, Europe, Asia and North America. All have well-developed limbs with four or five digits and movable eyelids; adults have fully functional lungs and no external gills. There are aquatic and terrestrial forms, but most are found in or near water, at least in the breeding season.

NAME: **Sharp-ribbed Salamander,** *Pleurodeles waltl*
RANGE: **Portugal and Spain (except N. and N. E.), Morocco**
HABITAT: **slow rivers, ponds, ditches**
SIZE: **15–30 cm (6–11¾ in)**

One of the largest European amphibians, the sharp-ribbed salamander has a stout body and a broad, flat head. Its skin is rough and there is a row of small protuberances along each side which lie at the tips of the ribs; the ribs are often distinct and may even protrude through the skin. A powerful swimmer, it is usually active at night, when it searches for small invertebrate animals to eat.

A courting male carries his mate on his back in the water before depositing his package of sperm on the bottom. He then lowers the female on to the sperm, and she collects it with her reproductive organ and is fertilized internally. She lays her eggs on a submerged stone.

NAME: **Fire Salamander,** *Salamandra salamandra*
RANGE: **central, W. and S. Europe; N. W. Africa, parts of S. W. Asia**
HABITAT: **forest on hills and mountains**
SIZE: **20–28 cm (7¾–11 in)**

A heavily built species with a rather short tail, the fire salamander is characterized by its bright markings, which may be in the form of spots or stripes. These markings provide warning to potential predators of the salamander's unpleasant body secretions, which irritate the mouth and eyes of enemies and may even be fatal to small mammals. Although a land-dweller, it prefers moist areas and is seldom far from water. It emerges from daytime refuges to hunt for its invertebrate prey at night.

Fire salamanders mate on land. The male carries the female around on his back, then deposits his sperm package on the ground and lowers her on to it. She collects the sperm with her reproductive organ and is fertilized internally. The eggs develop inside the female's body and, about 10 months after fertilization, she gives birth to 10 to 50 live young in the water.

NAME: **Warty Newt,** *Triturus cristatus*
RANGE: **Europe (not S. and S. W. France, Iberia, Ireland or S. Greece)**
HABITAT: **still or slow water, woodland**
SIZE: **14–18 cm (5½–7 in)**

A large, rough-skinned newt, the male develops a jagged crest on his back in the breeding season; females are often larger than males but do not develop crests. Warty newts feed on aquatic and land-living invertebrates and may also take small fish and other amphibians and their eggs.

The courting male performs an energetic display for his mate and then deposits sperm, over which the female walks or is led, and which she collects with her reproductive organ. She lays 200 to 300 eggs, one at a time, which hatch in 4 or 5 months.

NAME: **Eastern Newt,** *Notophthalmus viridescens*
RANGE: **S. E. Canada, E. USA: Great Lakes area to Florida and Texas**
HABITAT: **ponds and lakes with vegetation, ditches, swamps**
SIZE: **6.5–14 cm (2½–5½ in)**

The eastern newt occurs in several different patterns and colours over its wide range. Adults are aquatic and are eager predators, searching in shallow water for worms, insects, crustaceans and the eggs and young of other amphibians.

The breeding season begins in late winter or early spring. The female lays from 200 to 400 eggs, one at a time, on submerged plants and, after an incubation of up to 2 months, the eggs hatch into larvae. In later summer, these larvae transform into subadults, known as efts, and leave the water to spend up to 3 years living on land and feeding primarily on insects. They then return to the water and become mature, fully developed adults.

NAME: **Rough-skinned Newt,** *Taricha granulosa*
RANGE: **W. North America: Alaska to California**
HABITAT: **ponds, lakes, slow streams and surrounding grassland or woodland**
SIZES: **6.5–12.5 cm (2½–5 in)**

The most aquatic of Pacific newts, the rough-skinned newt is identified by its warty skin and its small eyes with dark lower lids. It searches for its invertebrate prey both on land and in the water, and its toxic skin secretions repel most of its enemies.

In the breeding season, the male's skin temporarily becomes smooth and his vent swells. Unlike other western newts, the female rough-skinned lays her eggs one at a time, rather than in masses, on submerged plants or debris. The eggs hatch in aquatic larae.

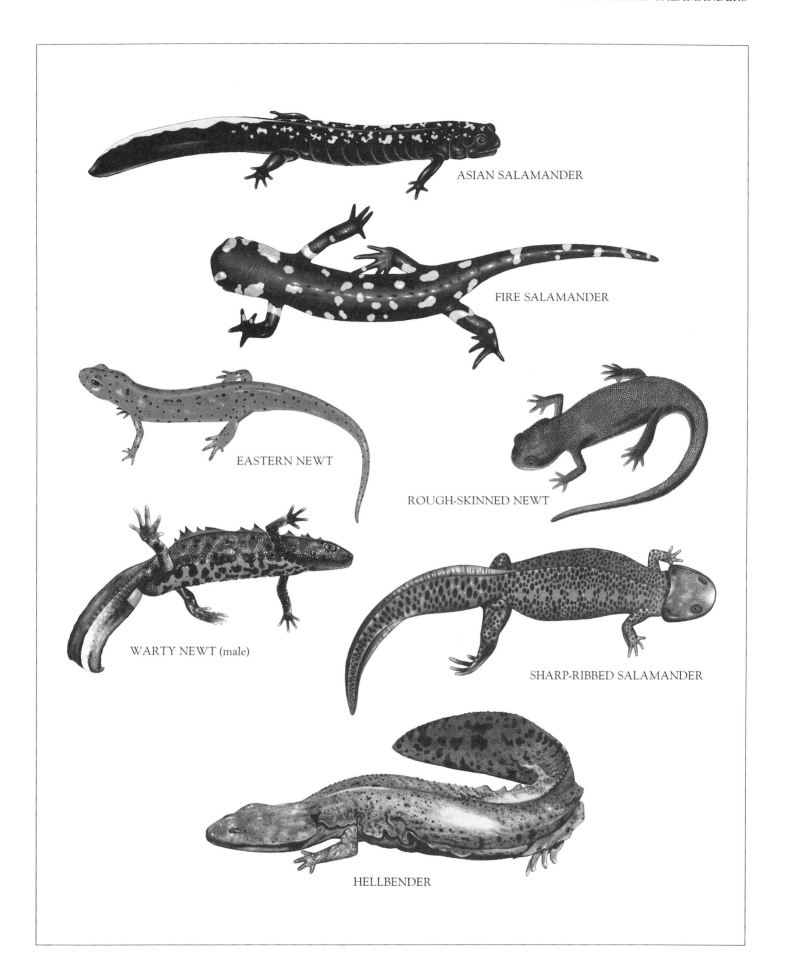

ASIAN SALAMANDER

FIRE SALAMANDER

EASTERN NEWT

ROUGH-SKINNED NEWT

WARTY NEWT (male)

SHARP-RIBBED SALAMANDER

HELLBENDER

Mole Salamanders

NAME: **Spotted Salamander,** *Ambystoma maculatum*
RANGE: **S. E. Canada, E. USA to Georgia and E. Texas**
HABITAT: **hardwood forest, hillsides near pools**
SIZE: **15–24 cm (6–9½ in)**

This stout-bodied salamander is identified by the irregular spots on its back, which run from head to tail. Rarely seen, it spends most of its life underground and feeds on slugs and worms.

In early spring, heavy rains stimulate the salamanders to migrate to breeding pools. The female lays about 100 eggs at a time, in a compact mass which adheres to submerged vegetation in the pond; she may lay more than one such mass. Some 4 to 8 weeks later, the eggs hatch into larvae 1.25 cm (½ in) long, which develop adult form at 2 to 4 months. Spotted salamanders may live for 20 years.

In some areas these salamanders are becoming rare because acid rain is polluting their breeding ponds and preventing the successful development of eggs. Acid rain contains dilute sulphur and nitric acids from the gases released into the atmosphere by the burning of fossil fuels and is a source of increasing anxiety to biologists. In the temporary rain and snow pools used by salamanders for breeding, acidity is often extremely high, causing a high failure rate of eggs and severe deformities in those young that do survive.

NAME: **Marbled Salamander,** *Ambystoma opacum*
RANGE: **E. USA: New Hampshire to Florida, west to Texas**
HABITAT: **woodland: swamp areas and drier, high ground**
SIZE: **9–12.5 cm (3½–5 in)**

A dark-coloured, stout species, the marbled salamander has some light markings that are the origin of its common name. The male's markings are brighter than the female's; juveniles are dark grey to brown with light flecks. The salamander emerges at night to hunt for slugs and worms but before morning hides under a log or stone where it remains for the day.

Marbled salamanders breed from September to December, depending on latitude, and mate and nest on land. The female lays 50 to 200 eggs, one at a time, in a dip on the ground that will later fill with rain. Until the rains come, the salamander curls itself round the eggs to protect them. The larvae hatch a few days after being covered by rain. If there is insufficient rainfall to fill the nest the eggs may not hatch until the spring. Once hatched, the larvae develop adult form at 4 to 6 months.

AMBYSTOMATIDAE:
Mole Salamander Family

There are about 32 species of mole salamander, all found in North America from Canada to Mexico. Typically, these salamanders have broad heads and a thick-bodied, sturdy appearance. Many species are ground-living, burrowing animals, rarely seen except in the breeding season when they migrate to ponds or streams to mate and lay eggs. Others have developed more aquatic habits and live in or near water most of the year. Larvae are aquatic and have feathery external gills and well-developed tail fins.

In most salamanders, the larvae remain permanently in the water while the adults spend at least part of the time on land. When the larva transforms into a mature, breeding adult, therefore, it loses such features as feathery external gills and the flattened tail, which are only useful in water. The mole salamander family is notable because some species can breed while still living in the water and still retaining these normally larval characteristics. This is known as neotenous breeding. Some geographical races of otherwise normal species are neotenous; for example, western forms of the North American tiger salamander, *Ambystoma tigrinum*, are neotenous, while the eastern relatives are normal.

Insects and small invertebrates are the main foods of all members of the family. Male and female mole salamanders look alike, but males usually have longer tails than females.

NAME: **Tiger Salamander,** *Ambystoma tigrinum*
RANGE: **S. central Canada, central USA, south to N. Florida and Mexico**
HABITAT: **arid plains, damp meadows, mountain forest**
SIZE: **15–40 cm (6–15¾ in)**

The world's largest land-dwelling salamander, the tiger salamander has a stout body, broad head and small eyes. Its coloration and pattern vary enormously, and it adapts to a wide variety of habitats, from sea-level to 3,350 m (11,000 ft). Tiger salamanders live near water among plant debris or use crayfish or mammal burrows for refuge. They are often active at night, particularly after heavy rain, and feed on earthworms, insects, mice and some small amphibians.

The timing of the breeding season varies according to area but it is usually prompted by rainfall. The salamanders mate in water and the female lays her eggs in masses which then adhere to submerged vegetation or debris.

NAME: **Axolotl,** *Ambystoma mexicanum*
RANGE: **Mexico: Lake Xochimilco**
HABITAT: **permanent water at high altitude**
SIZE: **up to 29 cm (11½ in)** ®

Now rare, the axolotl is threatened by the destruction of its habitat, the introduction of predatory fishes, such as carp, and the collection of specimens for the pet trade. A curious-looking creature, it has a dorsal fin, which extends from the back of its head to the tip and round the underside of its long tail, and three pairs of feathery external gills. Its legs and feet are small and weak. The name "axolotl" is an Aztec word meaning water monster.

Axolotls breed in water. The female is attracted to the male by the odour of the secretions of his abdominal glands. He fans his tail in her direction, thus sending the odour through the water. The female approaches and noses the male's glands. He then sheds his sperm in a small packet, known as a spermatophore, which sinks to the bottom of the water. The female settles over it and picks up the sperm packet with her cloaca (the external reproductive chamber) and is thus fertilized internally. In the wild, the axolotl lays about 400 eggs but may lay thousands in captivity.

The axolotl normally breeds neotenously (in the larval state), retaining its gills and remaining in water. However, some individuals do metamorphose into land-dwelling, gill-less adults.

NAME: **Pacific Giant Salamander,** *Dicamptodon ensatus*
RANGE: **Pacific coast of N. America: British Columbia to California; Idaho, Montana**
HABITAT: **cool, humid forest, rivers, streams and lakes**
SIZE: **7–30 cm (2¾–11¾ in)**

This smooth-skinned salamander is unusual in that it can make a low-pitched cry — most salamanders are silent. Adults live on land under logs, rocks and forest debris and may even climb into trees and bushes. Mainly active at night, they feed on snails, slugs, insects, mice and small snakes, and other salamanders.

In spring, adults breed in water, usually in the headwaters of a spring, and the female lays about 100 eggs on a submerged branch. The larvae live in cold clear lakes or streams; they are highly predatory and cannibalize smaller larvae, as well as feeding on tadpoles and insects. They may mature into adults in their second year or become sexually mature (neotenic) larvae when about 20 cm (7¾ in) long.

SPOTTED SALAMANDER

TIGER SALAMANDER

MARBLED SALAMANDER

PACIFIC GIANT SALAMANDER

AXOLOTL

Congo Eels, Olm and Mudpuppies, Sirens

AMPHIUMIDAE:
Congo Eel Family

The 3 species of elongate, eel-like creatures in this family are among the world's largest aquatic salamanders; they are all found in the southeastern USA. They have cylindrical bodies and tiny hind and forelimbs, each with one, two or three toes. These limbs are so small that it is doubtful whether they are of any use for locomotion. The skin of these amphibians is smooth and slippery.

Until 1950 there were thought to be only 2 species in this family, but a third species, the one-toed amphiuma, *Amphiuma pholeter*, was then discovered.

NAME: **Two-toed Congo Eel, *Amphiuma means***
RANGE: **USA: S. E. Virginia to Florida, E. Louisiana**
HABITAT: **swamps, bayous, drainage ditches**
SIZE: **45–116 cm (17$\frac{3}{4}$–45$\frac{1}{2}$ in)**

This aquatic salamander has tiny, virtually useless limbs, each with two toes. Mainly active at night, it hunts in water for crayfish, frogs, small snakes and fish and may come on to land in extremely wet weather. It takes refuge during the day in a burrow it digs in the mud or takes over the burrow of another creature.

Congo eels mate in water, and the female lays about 200 eggs in a beadlike string. The female coils around the eggs as they lie on the bottom and protects them until they hatch about 5 months after being laid. When the larvae hatch, they are about 5 cm (2 in) long; their tiny limbs are of more use to them at this stage than when they metamorphose to adult form, at about 7.5 cm (3 in) long. The three-toed amphiuma, *Amphiuma tridactylum*, also found in the southern USA, is similar in appearance and habits but has three toes on each of its tiny limbs.

PROTEIDAE:
Olm and Mudpuppy Family

There are 5 species of stream- and lake-dwelling mudpuppies in North America and 1 species of cave-dwelling olm in Europe. Because these amphibians live permanently in the water, they retain the external feathery gills throughout their lives, even into the adult breeding shape. They, therefore, resemble the larvae of other amphibians that do lose their gills when they become adult and leave water for at least part of the time.

NAME: **Olm, *Proteus anguinus***
RANGE: **Yugoslavia: E. Adriatic coast; N. E. Italy**
HABITAT: **streams and lakes in underground limestone caves**
SIZE: **20–30 cm (7$\frac{3}{4}$–11$\frac{3}{4}$ in)** (V)

The olm is a large aquatic salamander with a pale cylindrical body and red feathery gills. Its tail is flattened and its limbs weak and poorly developed. It has three toes on the forelimbs and two on the hind limbs. It lives in total darkness in its cave home and is virtually blind, its eyes hidden beneath the skin. It feeds on small aquatic worms and crustaceans.

The female olm lays 12 to 70 eggs at a time; the eggs are deposited under a stone and guarded by both parents. They hatch in about 90 days. Some females may reproduce in a different manner, retaining a small number of eggs inside the body and giving birth to 2 fully developed young. The young are miniature versions of the parents but have rudimentary eyes.

Once a common species, the olm is now becoming rare because of water pollution in its restricted habitat and the taking of large numbers for the pet trade.

NAME: **Mudpuppy, *Necturus maculosus***
RANGE: **S. Canada: Manitoba to Quebec; USA: Great Lakes, south to Georgia and Louisiana**
HABITAT: **lakes, rivers, streams**
SIZE: **20–43 cm (7$\frac{3}{4}$–17 in)**

An aquatic salamander, the mudpuppy inhabits a variety of freshwater habitats, from muddy, sluggish shallows to cold, clear water. It has four toes on each limb and a flattened tail. Its feathery gills vary in size according to the water the individual inhabits: mudpuppies in cold, well-oxygenated water have shorter gills than those in warm, muddy, poorly oxygenated water, which need large, bushy gills to collect all the available oxygen. It hunts worms, crayfish, insects and small fish, mainly at night, but may sometimes catch fish during the day.

The breeding season is from April to June. The female lays 30 to 190 eggs, each of which adheres separately to a log or rock. The male guards the eggs until they hatch some 5 to 9 weeks later. The larvae do not mature until they are 4 to 6 years old.

SIRENIDAE: Siren Family

The 3 species of sirens are aquatic salamanders which retain feathery external gills throughout life. Their bodies are long and eel-like and they have tiny forelimbs and no hind limbs. All species occur in the USA and northern Mexico.

Sirens swim by powerful undulations of the body and forage among water weeds for food; they are active at night. They breathe by means of external gills, positioned at each side of the neck.

NAME: **Dwarf Siren, *Pseudobranchus striatus***
RANGE: **USA: coastal plain of S. Carolina, Georgia, Florida**
HABITAT: **ponds, swamps, ditches**
SIZE: **10–25 cm (4–9$\frac{3}{4}$ in)**

The smallest of its family, the dwarf siren is a slender, eel-like creature which lives among dense submerged vegetation. It has no hind limbs and only tiny forelimbs with three toes on each foot. The external gills are retained throughout life. A nocturnal creature, the siren feeds on tiny invertebrate animals it finds among the plant debris near the bottom of the water. If its habitat is in danger of drying up, in a drought for example, the siren can burrow into the mud and remain there, dormant, for up to 2 months. Mucus produced by skin glands prevents the body drying out during such a period.

The females siren lays her eggs, one at a time, on aquatic plants and the larvae hatch out about 4 weeks later. There are about 5 races of dwarf siren over the range, which vary in coloration and in the shade and distribution of the stripes along the sides of the body.

NAME: **Greater Siren, *Siren lacertina***
RANGE: **USA: coastal plain from Virginia to Florida, S. Alabama**
HABITAT: **shallow, muddy fresh water with plenty of vegetation**
SIZE: **50–97.5 cm (19$\frac{3}{4}$–38$\frac{1}{4}$ in)**

The stout-bodied greater siren has permanent external gills and a flattened tail. There are four toes on each of its front feet. During the day it hides under rocks or plant debris or burrows into the muddy bottom, emerging at night to feed on snails, insect larvae, small fish and some aquatic plants. In drought conditions, the siren undergoes a period of dormancy; it seals itself in a cocoon made from secretions of the skin glands and buries itself in the muddy bottom until danger is past.

Sirens breed in February or March, laying eggs which hatch 2 or 3 months later into larvae which are about 1.25 cm ($\frac{1}{2}$ in) long.

DWARF SIREN

OLM

TWO-TOED CONGO EEL

MUDPUPPY

GREATER SIREN

Lungless Salamanders

NAME: **Texas Blind Salamander,**
Typhlomolge rathbuni
RANGE: **USA: extreme S. Texas**
HABITAT: **underground waters of the**
creek system
SIZE: **9–13.5 cm (3½–5¼ in)** Ⓔ

A rare species with an extremely restricted distribution, the Texas blind salamander is a typical cave-dweller, with its ghostly pale body and much-reduced eyes. Its external gills are red and feathery and it has long thin legs.

Many bats roost in the caves which are the only entrance to the salamanders' habitat. Nutrients in the droppings (guano) of these bats provide food for the invertebrate animals which inhabit the caves, and these creatures, many of which are unique, are in turn eaten by the salamanders.

Nothing is known at present about the breeding habits of this salamander.

NAME: **Red-backed Salamander,**
Plethodon cinereus
RANGE: **S. E. Canada, N. E. USA, south**
to North Carolina, S. Indiana
HABITAT: **cool, moist forest**
SIZE: **6.5–12.5 cm (2½–5 in)**

This abundant, widespread salamander lives its whole life on land. The "red back" of its common name is, in fact, a stripe which may vary greatly from red to grey or yellow; some forms have grey bodies and lack the stripe altogether. A nocturnal creature, it hides during the day under stones or forest litter and emerges at night to search for insects and small invertebrates.

Breeding takes place every other year. The salamanders court and mate during the winter, and in June or July the female lays her 6 to 12 eggs, which hang in a cluster in a crevice, under a rock or in a rotten log. She coils herself around the eggs and protects them until they hatch 8 or 9 weeks later. The larvae do not have an aquatic stage and take 2 years to reach maturity.

NAME: **Slimy Salamander, _Plethodon_**
glutinosus
RANGE: **E. and S. E. USA: New York to**
Florida, Missouri, Oklahoma
HABITAT: **floodplains, cave entrances**
SIZE: **11.5–20.5 cm (4½–8 in)**

A land-dwelling species, the slimy salamander's skin exudes a sticky substance that may have protective properties. By day, it shelters under rocks or logs or in a burrow, but at night, particularly after rain, it searches the forest floor for invertebrate prey.

Southern females breed every year, and northern females only every other year, laying 6 to 36 eggs in a burrow or in a rotten log and guarding them while they develop.

PLETHODONTIDAE:
Lungless Salamander Family

This, the most successful group of living salamanders, includes some 200 of the 300 or so known tailed amphibians. As their name suggests, these salamanders are primarily characterized by their total absence of lungs. The pulmonary artery, which would normally take blood to the lungs, is reduced to minute proportions in a lungless salamander and runs in the body wall. The animal obtains oxygen across its moist skin or through the internal surface of the mouth cavity, both of which are well supplied with blood vessels.

Nearly all lungless salamanders live in North or South America. Two species occur in Europe: the cave salamanders, found in Sardinia and mainland Italy. These forms can be distinguished from all other European salamanders by their partially webbed toes.

NAME: **Spring Salamander, _Gyrinophilus_**
porphyriticus
RANGE: **S. Canada: Quebec; USA: Maine,**
to Georgia, Mississippi
HABITAT: **wet caves, cool, clear mountain**
springs
SIZE: **10–22 cm (4–8¾ in)**

The spring salamander is one of the largest species in its family and occurs in several races, with variations of colour and pattern. It spends most of its life in water but on rainy nights may come on to land to search for food. Large insects, worms and other salamanders are its main prey.

In July or August, the female spring salamander lays 20 to 60 eggs, which are attached singly to the under-surfaces of submerged rocks. She guards the eggs for 3 months until they hatch. Larvae do not attain adult form and coloration for about 3 years.

NAME: **Red Salamander, _Pseudotriton_**
ruber
RANGE: **E. USA: S. New York, west to**
Indiana, south to Louisiana
HABITAT: **springs, surrounding**
woodland, swamps, meadows
SIZE: **9.5–18 cm (3¾–7 in)**

A brilliantly coloured species, the red salamander has a stout body and short tail and legs. It spends much of its life on land but usually in the vicinity of water. Earthworms, insects and small salamanders are its main foods.

After courting and mating in summer, the female red salamander lays 50 to 100 eggs in autumn. The larvae hatch in about 2 months and transform into adult form some 2 years later. Females first breed when 5 years old.

NAME: **Yellow-blotched Salamander,**
Ensatina eschscholtzi croceator
RANGE: **USA: California**
HABITAT: **moist forest, canyons**
SIZE: **7.5–15 cm (3–6 in)**

The yellow-blotched is one of several subspecies of _Ensatina_ with a wide variety of colours and patterns. All have the distinguishing feature of a tail which is constricted at its base. The male usually has a longer tail than the female. A land-dwelling species, it shelters under rocks and logs, making forays in search of spiders and large insects such as beetles and crickets.

The female lays from 7 to 25 eggs in spring or early summer in a burrow or rotting log. She guards the eggs while they develop. The larvae live on land and do not have an aquatic phase; they are mature at 2 to 3 years old.

NAME: **Dusky Salamander,**
Desmognathus fuscus
RANGE: **S. Canada; N. E. USA, south to**
Louisiana
HABITAT: **springs, woodland creeks,**
floodplains
SIZE: **6.5–14 cm (2½–5½ in)**

Young dusky salamanders have pairs of yellow or red spots on the back but, as they mature, these fade or become obscured. The dusky salamander can jump well when alarmed, leaping several times its own length to escape an enemy. It feeds mainly on insect larvae and earthworms.

In summer, the female lays 12 to 36 eggs in a cluster near water, usually under a rock or log. The larvae hatch in 2 to 3 months and reach maturity in 3 to 4 years.

NAME: **California Slender Salamander,**
Batrachoseps attenuatus
RANGE: **USA: S. W. Oregon, California,**
western slopes of Sierra Nevada
HABITAT: **redwood forest, grassland,**
mountains and foothills
SIZE: **7.5–14 cm (3–5½ in)**

True to its name, this salamander has a slim, elongate body and tail. Its legs and feet are tiny and narrow, with four toes on each foot. Coloration varies with area. The most common Californian salamander, it lives on land and moves with undulating movements of its body rather than by using its limbs. During the day, it hides in damp vegetation or among tree roots, and emerges at night to hunt for worms and spiders and other invertebrate prey. It is particularly active in rainy periods.

In late autumn or winter, stimulated by rainfall, the female lays 4 to 21 eggs under a rock or log. The eggs hatch in spring and the larvae do not undergo an aquatic phase.

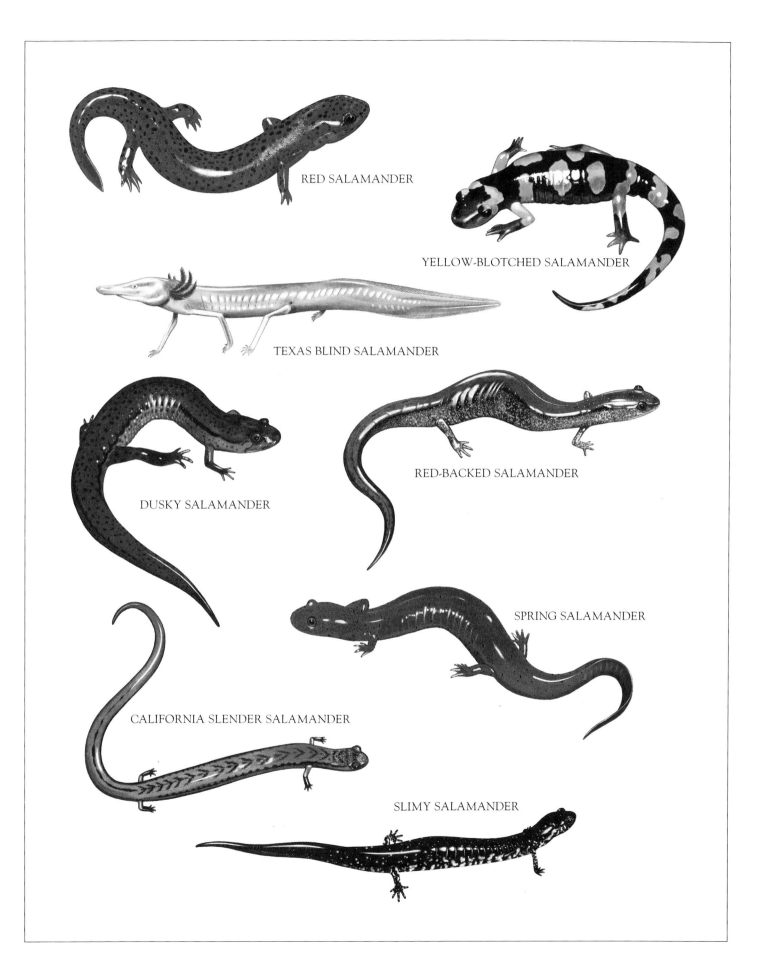

RED SALAMANDER

YELLOW-BLOTCHED SALAMANDER

TEXAS BLIND SALAMANDER

DUSKY SALAMANDER

RED-BACKED SALAMANDER

SPRING SALAMANDER

CALIFORNIA SLENDER SALAMANDER

SLIMY SALAMANDER

Caecilians

ORDER APODA

This order contains 4 families of caecilians, over 150 species in all. Caecilians are limbless amphibians with cylindrical, ringed bodies and resemble giant earthworms. One family is aquatic, but the others are blind, burrowing creatures, rarely seen above ground. They burrow into the rich, soft soil of tropical or warm temperate forests in search of their prey, usually earthworms, insects and other invertebrates. Adults have a sensory tentacle beneath each eye which is probably used for finding prey. Many species have small scales embedded in the surface of the skin. This is probably a primitive feature which all other amphibian groups have since lost.

CAECILIIDAE: Caecilian Family

There are 106 species in this family, all of which are land-dwelling burrowers. Many species have scales on the body. Females reproduce either by laying eggs, which develop and hatch outside the body, or by producing eggs, which are retained to develop and hatch inside the body, and are then born as live young. The young have external gills and may spend some time as free-swimming larvae. Species occur in Old and New World tropics.

NAME: **Panamanian Caecilian,** *Caecilia ochrocephala*
RANGE: **Central and South America: E. Panama, N. Colombia**
HABITAT: **forest**
SIZE: **up to 61 cm (24 in)**

The Panamanian caecilian has a small slender head and a wedge-shaped snout. It burrows into soft, usually moist, earth and seldom appears above ground except when heavy rains flush it from its burrow. It feeds mainly on insects and earthworms. Snakes often enter the burrows of these caecilians and devour them.

Little is known of the breeding habits of this rarely seen creature, but females are thought to lay eggs which then develop and hatch outside the body.

NAME: **South American Caecilian,** *Siphonops annulatus*
RANGE: **South America, east of Andes to Argentina**
HABITAT: **varied, often forest**
SIZE: **35 cm (13¾ in)**

This widespread caecilian has a short, thick body and no scales. It spends most of its life underground and feeds largely on earthworms. The female lays eggs, but it is not known whether the young pass through a larval stage.

NAME: **Sao Thomé Caecilian,** *Schistometopum thomensis*
RANGE: **Sao Thomé Island in Gulf of Guinea, off W. Africa**
HABITAT: **forest**
SIZE: **up to 30.5 cm (12 in)**

The body of this brightly coloured caecilian is usually about 1.25 cm (½ in) in diameter. Its snout is rounded and it has no tail. Like all caecilians, it lives underground, feeding on whatever invertebrate prey it can find, mainly on insects and worms. The female retains her eggs in her body where they develop and hatch; the young are then born in an advanced state of development.

NAME: **Seychelles Caecilian,** *Hypogeophis rostratus*
RANGE: **Seychelles**
HABITAT: **swampy coastal regions**
SIZE: **20 cm (7¾ in)**

The Seychelles caecilian has a slightly flattened body which tapers at both ends. The body colour darkens as the caecilian matures. It will burrow wherever the soil is moist and often lives beneath rocks or logs or even digs into rotting trees. It feeds on small invertebrates and on frogs such as *Sooglossus sechellensis*.

Mating takes place at any time of year when there is plenty of rain. The female lays 6 to 30 eggs, which are large and rich in yolk, and coils her body around them to guard them while they develop. The young do not pass through a larval stage but hatch as miniature adults.

ICHTHYOPHIDAE

There are 43 species in this family of terrestrial caecilians, found in Southeast Asia, Central America and tropical South America. They have short tails and scales on the body.

NAME: **Sticky Caecilian,** *Ichthyophis* **sp.**
RANGE: **S. E. Asia**
HABITAT: **forest**
SIZE: **up to 38 cm (15 in)**

Adult caecilians of this Southeast Asian genus live in burrows and feed on earthworms and small burrowing snakes. They breed in the spring. The female lays 20 or more eggs in a burrow she makes in moist ground near to water. She coils around her eggs while they develop, to protect them from predators. As they incubate, the eggs absorb moisture and gradually swell until they are double their original size. On hatching, the larva is four times the weight of a newly laid egg and has a pair of breathing pores on its head. The larvae undergo a prolonged aquatic phase before becoming land-based adults.

TYPHLONECTIDAE

There are 18 species of aquatic caecilian in this family, all found in tropical South America. They live in freshwater streams and ponds and, although they have no tails, the end of the body is laterally flattened for propulsion in water. Caecilians of this family lack the primitive body scales, present in other families.

NAME: *Typhlonectes compressicauda*
RANGE: **Guianas, Brazil**
HABITAT: **rivers, streams, pools**
SIZE: **52 cm (20½ in)**

Typical of its family, this aquatic caecilian swims with eel-like movements of its laterally compressed tail. Like all caecilians, male and female look similar, but the male has a protrusible copulatory organ with which he fertilizes his mate internally. The female retains her eggs inside her body while the young develop.

Having eaten all the yolk that surrounds them in their eggs, the young hatch and distribute themselves along the mother's oviduct. They feed on cells and drops of oil from the uterine wall which they obtain with the rasping plates in their mouths. More nutrients are obtained through the thin delicate skin which the young possess at this stage; they also have broad, baglike, external gills which disappear before they hatch. Once further development has taken place, the young are born; their thin skin is replaced by firmer, stronger skin, and the rasping plates by teeth.

SCOLECOMORPHIDAE

The 6 species of caecilian in this family are all of the same genus and occur only in central Africa. They are tail-less and have no primitive body scales. All species live on land in burrows.

NAME: *Scolecomorphus kirkii*
RANGE: **Africa: Tanzania, Malawi, Zambia**
HABITAT: **mountain forest**
SIZE: **up to 41 cm (16¼ in)**

This caecilian lives in burrows it digs under the leaf mould on the forest floor. Unlike other caecilians, it does not even come to the surface after rain. Termites and worms are its main foods.

Little is known of the breeding habits of this family. The male has a protrusible copulatory organ, and the female probably retains her eggs, which then develop inside her body like those of the *Typhlonectes* species, and hatch in an advanced state of development.

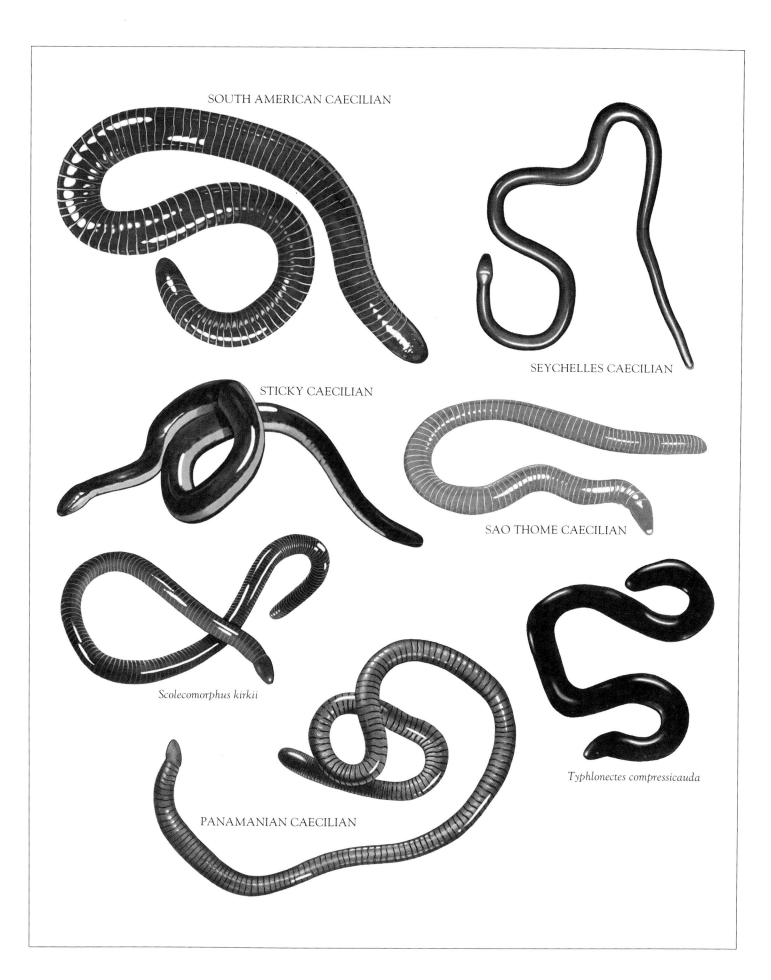

SOUTH AMERICAN CAECILIAN

SEYCHELLES CAECILIAN

STICKY CAECILIAN

SAO THOME CAECILIAN

Scolecomorphus kirkii

Typhlonectes compressicauda

PANAMANIAN CAECILIAN

Mexican Burrowing Toad, Pipid Frogs, Narrow-mouthed Frogs

ORDER ANURA

There are over 2,500 species of frog and toad, but all are similar in appearance whatever their habits. As adults they are tail-less and have well-developed limbs. Most breed in water, laying eggs which hatch into tailed tadpoles. The tadpoles live in water, feeding on vegetation, and later change to adult form.

The word "frog" was originally used only for members of the family Ranidae, and the word "toad" for members of the family Bufonidae. However, the two words are also used indiscriminately for members of other families, so there is now no taxonomic implication in their use.

RHINOPHRYNIDAE: Mexican Burrowing Toad Family

The single species in this family, the Mexican burrowing toad is highly specialized for a burrowing existence. It enters water only to breed.

NAME: **Mexican Burrowing Toad,** *Rhinophrynus dorsalis*
RANGE: **Mexico, Guatemala**
HABITAT: **woodland**
SIZE: **6.5 cm (2½ in)**

This unusual frog, equipped with horny, shovel-like appendages on its feet, is an expert burrower. At night, it emerges from its burrow to hunt for termites, which it licks up with its tongue.

When courting, the male frog makes guttural calls to attract a female. They mate in water; he clings to her back and, as she lays her eggs, fertilizes them. The tadpoles have sensory barbels around their mouths and lack the true lips possessed by most other tadpoles.

PIPIDAE: Pipid Frogs

There are 20 or more species of highly aquatic frogs in this family, found in Central and South America and in Africa, south of the Sahara. All have powerful hind limbs and large webbed hind feet but only small forelimbs and feet. As they swim, these forelimbs are held out in front of the head with the fingers spread as sensory probes, to search for food items.

NAME: **Surinam Toad,** *Pipa pipa*
RANGE: **N. South America**
HABITAT: **streams, rivers**
SIZE: **12–20 cm (4¾–7¾ in)**

This active, strong-swimming toad is a voracious predator and will eat almost anything it can find with its slender, tactile fingers, even carrion.

At the beginning of the Surinam toads' extraordinary mating ritual, the male clasps the female from the back, round her hind legs; this stimulates the skin on her back to swell. The clasped pair somersault through the water and, as they flip over, the female lays 3 to 10 eggs on the male's belly. He fertilizes the eggs and, still somersaulting, pushes them on to the female's back. This procedure is repeated until 40 to 100 eggs are laid. The eggs are enveloped in the swollen skin of the female's back, each in its own separate cell. Some 2 to 4 months later, they hatch into fully formed miniature toads.

NAME: **African Clawed Toad,** *Xenopus laevis*
RANGE: **South Africa**
HABITAT: **ponds, lakes**
SIZE: **6.5–12.5 (2½–5 in)**

This streamlined toad is as fast and agile in water as any fish and is even able to move backward. It can change its coloration from black to grey to mottled to match its background. The four digits on its forelimbs are tipped with claws, which it uses to forage in the mud for food, and it consumes any animal matter, even its own tadpoles.

The toads mate in water, the male making a soft buzzing sound under water to attract the female. The eggs, each enclosed in jelly, attach to submerged plants and hatch after 7 days.

MICROHYLIDAE: Narrow-mouthed Frog Family

There are 300 or more species of burrowing, terrestrial and tree-living frogs in this family, found in tropical regions all over the world and extending into temperate areas in North and South America. Tree-living forms are equipped with adhesive pads on finger- and toe-tips to aid climbing.

NAME: **Sheep Frog,** *Hypopachus cuneus*
RANGE: **USA: S. E. Texas; Mexico**
HABITAT: **margins of damp areas in arid country**
SIZE: **2.5–4.5 cm (1–1¾ in)**

A small, stout frog with a pointed snout, the sheep frog is a nocturnal species which hides during the day under rocks or debris or in a rodent burrow; at night it emerges to feed on ants and termites.

Sheep frogs mate at any time of year when stimulated by sufficient rainfall. The male attracts the female to the breeding pond by making his bleating call — the origin of the common name. He clasps the female's body, and her sticky body secretions help the pair to stay together while they lay and fertilize about 700 eggs.

NAME: **Eastern Narrow-mouthed Frog,** *Gastrophryne carolinensis*
RANGE: **S. E. USA: Missouri and Maryland, south to Florida, Gulf Coast and Texas**
HABITAT: **by ponds and ditches; under moist vegetation**
SIZE: **2–4 cm (¾–1½ in)**

An excellent burrower, this small, smooth-skinned frog can disappear into the soil in a moment. It rests in a burrow during the day and comes out at night to hunt for its insect food, mainly ants.

Breeding is stimulated by rainfall, sometime between April and October. The dark-throated male calls to the female, usually from water, and continues to call as they mate. The eggs float on the water surface for 3 days and then hatch into tadpoles.

NAME: **South African Rain Frog,** *Breviceps adspersus*
RANGE: **South Africa, Namibia, Botswana, Zimbabwe**
HABITAT: **savanna**
SIZE: **3 cm (1¼ in)**

An extremely rotund frog, the South African rain frog has a short snout and small, sturdy limbs. Its back is covered with warty protuberances and coloration and pattern are variable. It burrows well, using its hind feet, and seldom emerges above ground except during rain. It feeds on insects and small invertebrates.

The courting male makes a repeated croaking chirp to attract his mate. They mate in a burrow, held together by sticky body secretions. The few eggs are enclosed in thick jelly and lie in a compact mass in the burrow while they develop. There is no tadpole stage; metamorphosis takes place within the egg capsules and the young hatch as miniature, land-living frogs.

NAME: **Termite Frog,** *Phrynomerus bifasciatus*
RANGE: **Africa, south of the Sahara**
HABITAT: **savanna**
SIZE: **5 cm (2 in)**

The termite frog has a more elongate body than most members of its family and an unusually mobile head. Its distinctive markings warn of its toxic skin which contains substances which irritate the skin and mucuous membranes of predators. A land-dwelling frog, it may climb up tree stumps and rocks or burrow in search of prey or to shelter from dry weather. Termites and ants are its main foods.

Breeding takes place in shallow pools. The small, jelly-coated eggs are laid in masses and attach to submerged plants or lie at the bottom of the water. They hatch into aquatic tadpoles.

AFRICAN CLAWED TOAD

MEXICAN BURROWING TOAD

EASTERN NARROW-MOUTHED FROG

SURINAM TOAD

SOUTH AFRICAN RAIN FROG

TERMITE FROG

SHEEP FROG

Discoglossid Frogs, Tailed Frogs, Spadefoot Toads

DISCOGLOSSIDAE:
Discoglossid Frog Family

The 12 species in this family include the fire-bellied toads, painted frogs and midwife toads, all of which live in the Old World — in Europe, North Africa and parts of Asia. They are characterized by their disc-shaped tongues, which are entirely joined to the floor of the mouth and cannot be flipped forward to capture prey. Most frogs have tongues which are fixed only at the front, leaving the back free to be swiftly flipped over and protruded.

NAME: **Midwife Toad,** *Alytes obstetricans*
RANGE: **W. Europe, south to Alps, Spain and Portugal**
HABITAT: **woodland, cultivated land**
SIZE: **up to 5 cm (2 in)**

The small, plump midwife toad varies in coloration from grey to olive-green or brown, often with darker markings. A nocturnal, land-dwelling animal, it hides by day in crevices in walls or quarries or under logs. Some individuals live in burrows, which they dig with their strong forelimbs. Midwife toads feed on insects and small invertebrates.

The midwife toad is best known for its unusual breeding habits. The toads mate on land at night, the male clasping the female as she lays strings of up to 60 eggs. Once he has fertilized the eggs, he inserts his hind legs among them and twists the strings of eggs around his legs. He carries the eggs in this way while they develop, taking care that they do not dry out and moistening them at intervals in pools. After 18 to 49 days, depending on the temperature, the male deposits his eggs in shallow water, where they hatch into tadpoles.

NAME: **Oriental Fire-bellied Toad,** *Bombina orientalis*
RANGE: **Siberia, N. E. China, Korea**
HABITAT: **mountain streams, rice fields**
SIZE: **5 cm (2 in)**

A brilliantly coloured species, the oriental fire-bellied toad's rough skin exudes a milky secretion which is extremely irritating to the mouths and eyes of predators.

The female toad lays her eggs on the underside of submerged stones in small clumps, each containing 2 to 8 eggs.

ASCAPHIDAE: Tailed Frog Family

There are only 4 species in this family, 3 in New Zealand and 1 in North America. Despite their name, they do not have true tails but all possess tail-wagging muscles.

NAME: **Hochstetter's Frog,** *Leiopelma hochstetteri*
RANGE: **New Zealand**
HABITAT: **mountains, mountain streams**
SIZE: **4.5 cm (1¾ in)** ®

The 3 species in the genus *Leiopelma* are the only native frogs in New Zealand, and all are now rare and rigorously protected. Other frogs on the islands are introduced species.

First discovered in 1852, Hochstetter's frog is a robust species with partially webbed hind feet. Although it usually lives in or near water, it has also been found in mountain country some distance from streams. Like its relatives, it is nocturnal and feeds on beetles, ants, earthworms, spiders and slugs.

The breeding habits of this frog are probably an adaptation to its habitat. Groups of 2 to 8 eggs are laid on moist earth under logs or stones, or in tunnels left by dragonfly nymphs. Each egg is surrounded by a water-filled gelatinous capsule and, within this capsule, the embryo passes through all the tadpole stages until it hatches out as a tiny tailed froglet, about 40 days after laying. The tail is resorbed about a month later.

NAME: **Tailed Frog,** *Ascaphus truei,*
RANGE: **Pacific coast of N. America**
HABITAT: **mountain streams, damp forest**
SIZE: **2.5–5 cm (1–2 in)**

The male tailed frog has a unique tail-like structure which is, in fact, a copulatory organ for internal fertilization of the female. He clasps the female round the waist and deposits sperm directly into her cloaca. She then lays her eggs in a stream, where they attach to rocks. When the tadpoles hatch, they will cling to rocks or any other object with their strong, sucking mouthparts, to avoid being swept away by strong currents. The tadpoles feed on tiny plants and animals and metamorphose to adult form in 1 to 3 years.

PELOBATIDAE:
Spadefoot Toad Family

The 54 species of spadefoot toad are found in North America, Europe, North Africa and southern Asia. Many are highly terrestrial and nocturnal, spending their days in underground burrows. They are known as spadefoots because of the horny tubercle, found on the inner edge of each hind foot, which is used as a digging tool.

Spadefoots breed rapidly after rains, in temporary rainpools. Because the pools will soon dry up, development must be accelerated and eggs may hatch, pass though the tadpole stage and metamorphose in 2 weeks.

NAME: **European Spadefoot,** *Pelobates fuscus*
RANGE: **W., central and E. Europe to W. Asia**
HABITAT: **sandy soil, cultivated land**
SIZE: **up to 8 cm (3¼ in)**

The plump, European spadefoot has a large, pale-coloured spade on each virtually fully webbed hind foot. Males are usually smaller than females and have raised oval glands on their upper forelimbs. Like most spadefoots, this species is nocturnal outside the breeding season.

In the breeding season, however, spadefoots may be active during the day. They breed once a year in spring, usually in deep pools or in ditches. Although spadefoots do not develop the rough nuptial pads which males of many other families have to help them grasp their mates, they clasp the females and fertilize the eggs as they are laid.

NAME: **Western Spadefoot,** *Scaphiopus hammondi*
RANGE: **W. U.S.A: California, Arizona, New Mexico; Mexico**
HABITAT: **varied, plains, sandy areas**
SIZE: **3.5–6.5 cm (1¼–2½ in)**

An expert burrower, the western spadefoot has a wedge-shaped spade on each hind foot. It is a nocturnal toad and spends the day in its burrow in conditions of moderate temperature and humidity, despite the arid heat typical of much of its range.

Temporary rainpools are used for breeding, any time between January and August, depending on rainfall. The eggs are laid in round clumps which attach to vegetation and hatch only 2 days later. Since development must be completed before the temporary pool dries up, metamorphosis from tadpole to adult form takes place in under 6 weeks.

NAME: **Parsley Frog,** *Pelodytes punctatus*
RANGE: **Europe: Spain, Portugal, France, W. Belgium, N. Italy**
HABITAT: **various damp areas**
SIZE: **up to 5 cm (2 in)**

A nocturnal, mainly terrestrial creature outside the breeding season, the parsley frog is often found among vegetation near streams or by walls. It is a small, active frog with warty skin and virtually unwebbed hind feet. Parsley frogs climb, swim and jump well and can dig shallow burrows, despite the fact that they lack the spadelike hind foot appendages characteristic of the family.

Parsley frogs mate in spring and may breed more than once a season. Bands of eggs, held together by a thick gelatinous substance, twine round submerged vegetation, where they remain until they hatch into tadpoles.

HOCHSTETTER'S FROG

ORIENTAL FIRE-BELLIED TOAD

EUROPEAN SPADEFOOT

TAILED FROG

PARSLEY FROG

MIDWIFE TOAD

(male with eggs)

WESTERN SPADEFOOT

Myobatrachid Frogs, Ghost Frogs, Leptodactylid Frogs, Mouth-brooding Frog

MYOBATRACHIDAE:
Myobatrachid Frog Family
The species in this small family of frogs appear to have affinities with the bufonid toads and were previously classified with them. Members of the family tend to walk rather awkwardly, on the tips of their toes.

NAME: **Corroboree Frog,** *Pseudophryne corroboree*
RANGE: **Australia: Victoria, New South Wales**
HABITAT: **mountain forest, grassy marshland**
SIZE: **3 cm (1¼ in)**

A most distinctive species, the corroboree frog has a bright yellow body, patterned with irregular black stripes. It lives on land but near water, often at altitudes of more than 1,500 m (5,000 ft), and shelters under logs or in a burrow, which it digs itself.

In summer, the frogs seek out sphagnum bogs, where they dig nesting burrows. Up to 12 large eggs are laid in a burrow and one parent usually remains with the eggs while they develop. The tadpoles remain in the eggs until there is sufficient rainfall to wash them into a creek, where they hatch at once.

NAME: *Cyclorana cultripes*
RANGE: **Australia: N. coasts, Western Australia to Queensland**
HABITAT: **underground**
SIZE: **5 cm (2 in)**

This burrowing frog emerges above ground only to breed and to find some of its food — mostly insects and larvae. It has a strong, fairly stout body with warty skin and irregular dark patches on its back.

It breeds after heavy summer rain storms, often in temporary ponds or swollen creeks. The eggs are laid in the water, where they attach to submerged plants until they hatch into fat tadpoles with pointed snouts and deep tail fins.

HELEOPHRYNIDAE:
Ghost Frog Family
Ghost frogs are so called not because of any spectral appearance but because a species was discovered in Skeleton Gorge in South Africa. About 3 or 4 species are known, all found in southern Africa in fast-flowing mountain streams. They are long-limbed frogs with flattened bodies, enabling them to squeeze into narrow rock crevices, and expanded digits with which to grip slippery surfaces.

NAME: **Natal Ghost Frog,** *Heleophryne natalensis*
RANGE: **N. E. South Africa**
HABITAT: **forested streams**
SIZE: **up to 5 cm (2 in)**

A nocturnal species, the ghost frog takes refuge by day among rocks and pebbles or in crevices, concealed by its mottled, speckled coloration.

In the breeding season, male frogs develop nuptial pads on the forelimbs and small spines on the fingers and armpits for grasping their mates. The eggs are laid in a pool or even out of the water on wet gravel. Once hatched, tadpoles move to fast-flowing streams where they can withstand the currents by holding on to stones with their suckerlike mouths.

LEPTODACTYLIDAE:
Leptodactylid Frog Family
This is a large and varied family with several hundred species, found mainly in Central and South America, Africa and Australia. Their anatomy is similar to that of the true treefrogs (Hylidae), but although the Leptodactylid frogs may have adhesive discs on the digits, they lack the internal structure which makes the treefrogs' digits so flexible.

NAME: **Horned Frog,** *Ceratophrys cornuta*
RANGE: **N. and central South America**
HABITAT: **litter on forest floor**
SIZE: **20 cm (7¾ in)**

The extremely stout horned frog is almost as broad as it is long and has a wide, powerful head and large mouth. The eyes are relatively small, with a small protuberance on each upper eyelid. The toes are partially webbed, although the frog spends much of its life half-buried in the ground. Snails, small frogs and rodents are all eaten by this robust frog, and it is believed to cannabalize the young of its own species.

NAME: **Glass Frog,** *Centrolenella albomaculata*
RANGE: **N. South America**
HABITAT: **forest**
SIZE: **up to 3 cm (1¼ in)**

The glass frog behaves much like the hylid treefrogs and lives in small trees and bushes, usually near running water. Its digits are expanded into adhesive discs which give a good grip when it is climbing.

Eggs are laid in clusters on the underside of leaves overhanging running water and are guarded by the male. The tadpoles hatch and tumble down into the water below, where they complete their development.

NAME: **South American Bullfrog,** *Leptodactylus pentadactylus*
RANGE: **Central and South America: Costa Rica to Brazil**
HABITAT: **forest, close to water**
SIZE: **up to 20.5 cm (8 in)**

The largest species in its family, the South American bullfrog has particularly powerful hind legs, which are eaten by man in some parts of its range. The male has hard protuberances on each thumb and powerful arm muscles, both of which help him hold the female when mating. The female has ridged horny structures on her body into which the male's thumb-horns fit.

In the spawning season, the sides of the bullfrog's legs turn deep orange or red. The frogs mate in water; the male clasps the female, who secretes a jellylike substance which he then whips into a foam. The foam forms a nest which floats on or near the water surface and in which the eggs are laid and fertilized. Once they hatch, the tadpoles remain within the protection of the nest until, having metamorphosed into adults, they wriggle out into the water.

RHINODERMATIDAE:
Mouth-brooding Frog Family
This South American family, probably closely related to the Leptodactylidae, contains the unusual mouth-brooding, or Darwin's, frog of the genus *Rhinoderma*. Males of this species carry the developing eggs, and then the tadpoles, in their vocal sacs until they transform into small frogs. The species was discovered by Charles Darwin.

NAME: **Darwin's Frog,** *Rhinoderma darwinii*
RANGE: **S. Chile, S. Argentina**
HABITAT: **shallow, cold streams in forest**
SIZE: **3 cm (1¼ in)**

A small, slender frog, Darwin's frog has a pointed extension of skin on its head. Its digits are long and webbed on the hind feet but free on the forefeet.

The breeding habits of *Rhinoderma* are unique among amphibians. The female lays from 20 to 45 eggs on land. They are guarded by several males for 10 to 20 days until the embryos, which are visible from the outside, begin to move around inside the capsules. Each male then gathers up to 15 eggs with his tongue and lets them slide into his large vocal sac. The tadpoles develop inside the sac, which expands as they grow, feeding on their own yolks. Once they have transformed into small adults about 1.25 cm (½ in) long, the male expels them into water, and his vocal sac shrinks back to its normal size.

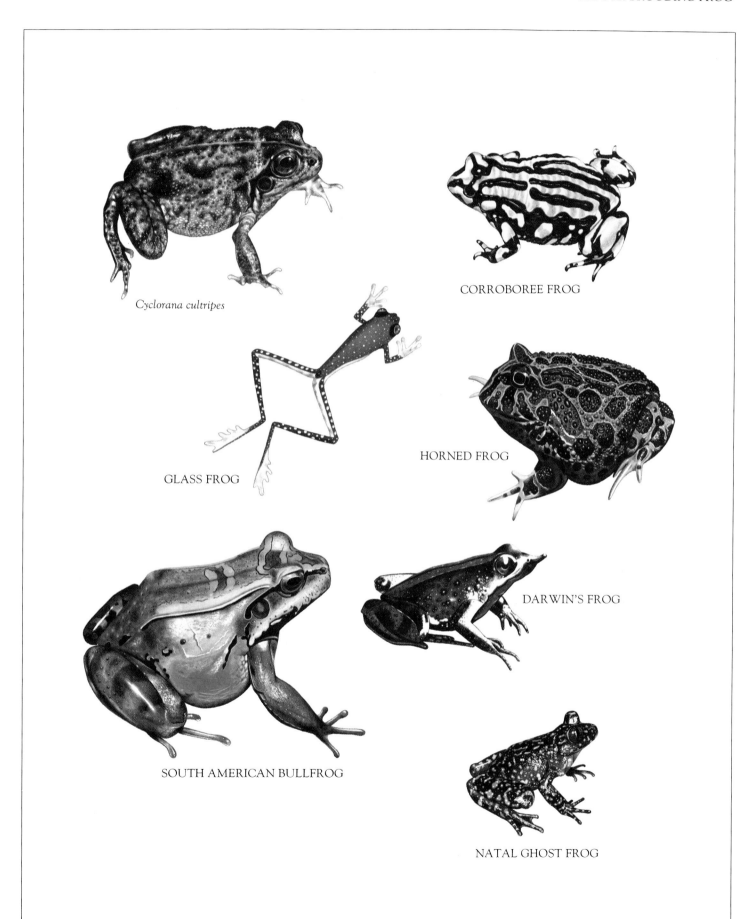

Cyclorana cultripes

CORROBOREE FROG

GLASS FROG

HORNED FROG

DARWIN'S FROG

SOUTH AMERICAN BULLFROG

NATAL GHOST FROG

Bufonid Toads, Gold Frog

BUFONIDAE: Toad Family

The name "toad" was originally applied only to the approximately 300 species in this family, although many other anurans with warty skins and terrestrial habits tend to be called toads. Bufonid toads are found over most of the world, except in the far north, Madagascar and Polynesia. A species has now been introduced into Australia, where previously there were no bufonid toads.

The typical bufonid toad has a compact body and short legs. The skin is not moist and is covered with characteristic wartlike tubercles. These contain the openings of poison glands, the distasteful secretions of which protect the toads to some extent, particularly from mammalian predators. With their short legs, toads tend to walk rather than hop and are, in general, slower-moving than frogs. Breeding males develop rough nuptial pads on their three inner fingers for clasping females when mating.

NAME: **Boulenger's Arrow Poison Toad,** *Atelopus boulengeri*
RANGE: **South America: Ecuador, Peru**
HABITAT: **forested slopes of the Andes, near fast-flowing streams**
SIZE: **about 2.5 cm (1 in)**

The contrasting black and orange markings of this toad warn of the poisonous skin secretions that defend it from predators. An uncommon, slow-moving species, it is active during the day and may climb up into bushes at night.

Little is known of its breeding habits, but it is believed to lay its eggs under stones in streams. The tadpoles probably have sucking mouths to anchor themselves to rocks in the fast-flowing water.

NAME: **American Toad,** *Bufo americanus*
RANGE: **S. E. Canada: Manitoba to Labrador, south to Great Lakes; USA: south to Georgia, east to Kansas**
HABITAT: **grassland, forest, gardens**
SIZE: **5–11 cm (2–4¼ in)**

A stout, broad-headed toad, the American toad is liberally covered with warts. Females are usually larger than males. Mainly nocturnal, the American toad takes refuge during the day under stones, logs or other debris or burrows into the soil. It feeds on insects, but also eats small invertebrates such as spiders, snails and earthworms.

American toads usually breed between March and July in ponds or streams. The female lays two strings of spawn, each containing up to 8,000 eggs, which hatch into tadpoles in 3 to 12 days. The tadpoles metamorphose into adults about 2 months after hatching.

NAME: **Giant Toad,** *Bufo marinus*
RANGE: **USA: extreme S. Texas; Mexico to Central and South America; introduced in many areas, including Australia**
HABITAT: **varied, near pools, swamps**
SIZE: **10–24 cm (4–9½ in)**

One of the largest toads in the world, the giant toad has been introduced widely outside its range, often to feed on, and thus control, insects which destroy crops such as sugar. It adapts well to many habitats and feeds on almost anything, including small rodents and birds and many insects, particularly beetles. Toxic secretions from the glands at each side of its body are highly irritating to mucous membranes and may be fatal to mammalian predators.

Giant toads breed at any time of year, given sufficient rainfall and warmth. They lay their strings of eggs in permanent water, where they usually hatch into tadpoles in 3 days. One female may lay up to 35,000 eggs in a year.

NAME: **Green Toad,** *Bufo viridis*
RANGE: **Europe: S. Sweden through Germany to Italy and Mediterranean islands; N. Africa, central Asia**
HABITAT: **varied, often lowland sandy areas, not forest**
SIZE: **8–10 cm (3¼–4 in)**

A thickset species but less plump than the common toad, the green toad has warty skin and distinctive green markings. The female is larger than the male, with brighter markings, and the male has an external vocal sac. Green toads are mainly nocturnal, but they may occasionally emerge during the day to forage for their insect food. Although primarily a land-living toad, the green toad has partially webbed toes and can survive in even brackish water.

Green toads breed from April to June, males courting females with their trilling, musical calls. The mating male clasps the female under her armpits while she lays two long strings of gelatinous spawn, each containing 10,000 to 20,000 eggs.

NAME: **Natterjack Toad,** *Bufo calamita*
RANGE: **W. and central Europe (including Britain), east to Russia**
HABITAT: **varied, often sandy areas**
SIZE: **7–10 cm (2¾–4 in)**

The male natterjack has the loudest call of any European toad: his croak will carry 2 km (1¼ mls) or more. The female is usually larger than the male, but both are robust and relatively short-limbed. Although mainly terrestrial, natterjacks are often found near the sea and may even use brackish water for breeding. They move on land by running in short spurts and are most active at night.

The breeding season lasts from March to August. Natterjacks mate at night and the female lays several strings of gelatinous spawn, each containing up to 4,000 eggs, in shallow water. The eggs hatch in 10 days into tadpoles which metamorphose to adult form in 4 to 8 weeks. The young frogs are not fully grown and mature until they are 4 or 5 years old.

NAME: **Common Toad,** *Bufo bufo*
RANGE: **Europe (including Britain and Scandinavia); N. Africa, N. Asia to Japan**
HABITAT: **varied, often fairly dry**
SIZE: **up to 15 cm (6 in)**

The largest European toad, the common toad varies in size over its wide range, but females are generally larger than males. It is a heavily built toad with extremely warty skin; males do not have external vocal sacs. A nocturnal species, it hides during the day, often using the same spot time after time, and emerges at dusk to feed on a variety of invertebrate prey. It usually moves by walking but, if distressed, may hop.

In much of their range, common toads hibernate in winter and then congregate in large numbers to breed at about the end of March, frequently returning to the same pond every year. Thousands of eggs are laid in gelatinous strings up to 3 m (10 ft) long. The eggs hatch in about 10 days and, if the weather is warm, the tadpoles metamorphose in about 2 months. In cold weather they take longer.

BRACHYCEPHALIDAE: Gold Frog Family

Closely related to the bufonid toads is the single species of frog in this family, the gold frog.

NAME: **Gold Frog,** *Brachycephalus ephippium*
RANGE: **South America: S. E. Brazil**
HABITAT: **mountain forest**
SIZE: **up to 2 cm (¾ in)**

This tiny, but exquisite, frog is common among the leaf litter of the forest floor, although it may hide in crevices in trees or rocks in dry weather. On its back is a bony shield, made of hard plates fused to the spines of the vertebrae. The frog may use this shield to block the entrance of its hiding place, so maintaining its humidity.

Its breeding habits are unknown but, since the tadpoles are aquatic, it is presumed that the frog lays its eggs in or near water.

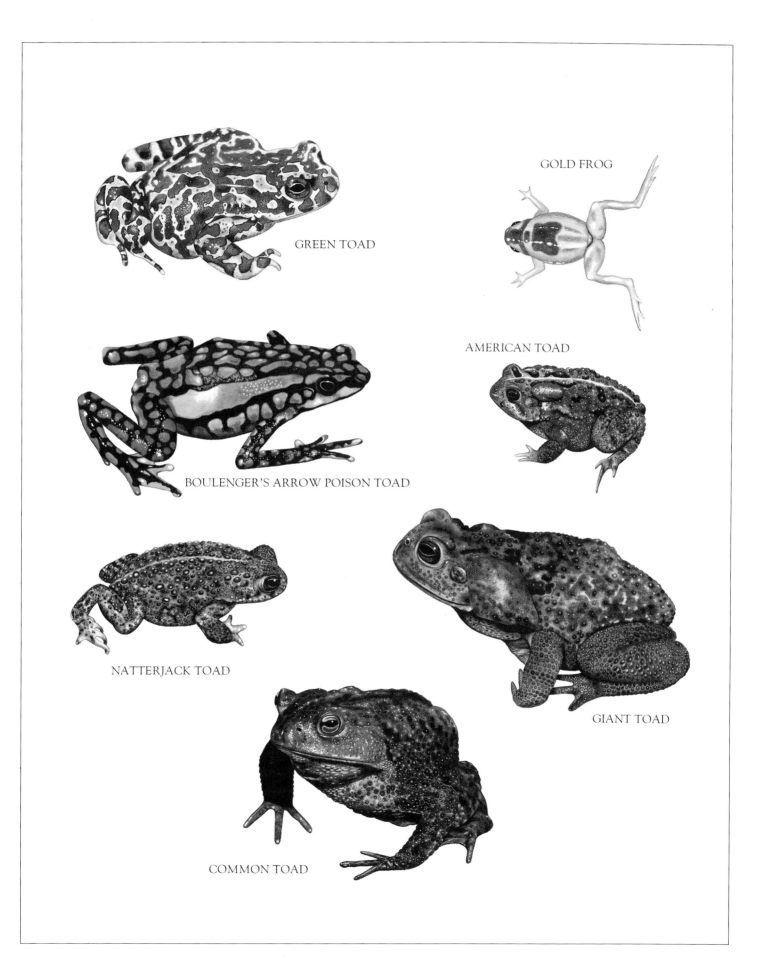

GREEN TOAD

GOLD FROG

AMERICAN TOAD

BOULENGER'S ARROW POISON TOAD

NATTERJACK TOAD

GIANT TOAD

COMMON TOAD

Treefrogs

NAME: **European Green Treefrog,** *Hyla arborea*
RANGE: **most of Europe except N. and parts of S. France and Spain; Turkey, S. USSR to Caspian Sea**
HABITAT: **bushes, trees, reeds near ponds and lakes**
SIZE: **up to 5 cm (2 in)**

The most arboreal of European amphibians, this smooth-skinned treefrog spends most of its life in trees where it captures flying insects with great skill. It can change colour rapidly, from bright green in sunlight to a dark grey in shade.

In early summer, breeding frogs congregate at night in ponds or other small areas of fresh water. The male grasps the female just behind the forelegs and fertilizes her eggs as they are shed into the water. The eggs are laid in clumps of up to 1,000 and float on the water until they hatch into tadpoles.

NAME: **Common Grey Treefrog,** *Hyla versicolor*
RANGE: **S. E. Canada; USA: N. Dakota, east to Maine, south to Texas and Florida**
HABITAT: **bushes, trees near water**
SIZE: **3–6 cm (1¼–2¼ in)**

A rough-skinned frog, the grey treefrog's variable coloration gives good camouflage in trees, and the bright orange areas on the under-surfaces of its thighs can be fleetingly flashed to confuse predators. It lives high up in vegetation and is mainly active at night, when it preys on insects.

Rarely seen on the ground, these treefrogs usually descend only to call and breed. They mate in water and the eggs are shed in small clusters of 10 to 40. The tadpoles hatch 4 or 5 days later.

NAME: **Spring Peeper,** *Hyla crucifer*
RANGE: **S. E. Canada; USA, south to central Florida, west to Texas**
HABITAT: **woodland, near ponds, swamps**
SIZE: **2–3 cm (¾–1¼ in)**

One of the most abundant frogs in eastern North America, the spring peeper's song does indeed herald the arrival of spring in the north of its range. This agile little frog can climb into trees and bushes, using its well-developed adhesive toe pads, and jump over 17 times its body length. It feeds mainly on small spiders and insects, including flying insects which it leaps into the air to catch.

Courting males call from trees overhanging water, making a bell-like chorus. The male frog climbs on to a female who enters water and lays her 800 to 1,000 eggs, one at a time, on to stems of aquatic vegetation. He fertilizes the eggs which hatch within a few days. The tadpoles metamorphose about 3 months later and leave the pond.

HYLIDAE: Treefrog Family

There are approximately 600 species of treefrog, found on all continents except the Antarctic, but the greatest diversity occurs in tropical areas of the New World. The vast majority live in trees and they possess a range of anatomical and behavioural adaptations which make them extremely efficient insect-eating, tree-dwelling amphibians.

The most important of these adaptations are on the feet. Each digit is tipped with a sticky adhesive pad to aid climbing, and inside the digit is a disc-shaped zone of cartilage before the claw-shaped end bone. The cartilage allows the digit great mobility, while keeping the adhesive pad flat on the surface which the frog is climbing.

NAME: **Northern Cricket Frog,** *Acris crepitans*
RANGE: **USA: New York, south to N. Florida, west to Minnesota and Texas**
HABITAT: **shallow ponds, slow streams**
SIZE: **1.5–4 cm (½–1½ in)**

This tiny rough-skinned frog is a poor climber and spends its life on land and in water. Unlike the arboreal treefrogs which do not jump readily, the cricket frog leaps and hops along and can jump as much as 36 times its own length.

Breeding starts in April in the north of its range or as early as February in the south. Thousands of frogs congregate to call and mate — the male's call is a shrill, metallic clicking sound. The eggs are shed on submerged vegetation or into the water in small clusters or singly. In warm weather, they hatch in 4 days but may take longer if the temperature is below 22°C (72°F).

NAME: **Golden Arrow-poison Frog,** *Dendrobates auratus*
RANGE: **Central and South America: Nicaragua to Panama and Colombia**
HABITAT: **forest**
SIZE: **4 cm (1½ in)**

The brilliant colours of this ground-dwelling frog warn potential enemies of its poisonous glandular secretions. This poison is extracted by local tribesmen and used on the tips of arrows.

Before mating, these frogs fight and contest with each other until they have paired. The female then lays up to 6 eggs, surrounded with a gelatinous substance, on land. The male visits the clutch at intervals until, about 2 weeks after laying, the tadpoles hatch. They then wriggle on to the male frog's back and he carries them to a hole in a tree where a little water has collected. Here, the aquatic tadpoles complete their development in about 6 weeks.

NAME: **Green and Gold Bell Frog,** *Litoria cyclorhynchus*
RANGE: **W. Australia: south coast**
HABITAT: **large ponds**
SIZE: **up to 8 cm (3¼ in)**

A distinctively marked species, this bell frog climbs only rarely and lives mostly in water or on reeds. It moves on land only in heavy rainfall. Active during the day, it is a voracious predator, feeding on any small animals, including its own tadpoles.

In the breeding season, males call from the water to attract mates, making a sound rather like wood being sawn. The female lays her eggs among the vegetation in the pond.

NAME: **Lutz's Phyllomedusa,** *Phyllomedusa appendiculata*
RANGE: **South America: S. E. Brazil**
HABITAT: **forest, near moving water**
SIZE: **4 cm (1½ in)**

A tree-dwelling frog, Lutz's phyllomedusa has triangular flaps of skin on each heel, which may help to camouflage its outline as it sits on a branch. Areas of red skin inside thighs and flanks can be flashed to confuse predators. It feeds mainly on insects.

The breeding method of this species is an adaptation to arboreal life. The breeding pair selects a leaf which overhangs water. They fold the leaf over, making a nest which is open at both sides, and the 50 or so eggs are laid in a ball of gelatinous mucus inside the nest. When the tadpoles hatch 2 or 3 days later, they drop into the water below.

NAME: **Marsupial Frog,** *Gastrotheca marsupiata*
RANGE: **South America: Ecuador, Peru**
HABITAT: **forest**
SIZE: **up to 4 cm (1½ in)**

This tree-dwelling frog is typical of its family in most respects but has the most extraordinary way of caring for its developing eggs. The female frog is larger than the male and has a special skin pouch on her back. While she lays about 200 eggs, one at a time, the male sits on her back. As each egg is laid, she bends forward so that it rolls down her back; the male then fertilizes the egg before it settles into the skin pouch. When all the eggs are laid, the male helps to pack them into the skin pouch and the edges of the pouch seal over.

A few weeks later the female frog finds some shallow water — a pond or puddle — in which to release her brood. By this time her back is very swollen. She raises one hind leg and, with her fourth and longest toe, slits open the pouch and frees the young tadpoles which then complete their metamorphosis in water.

COMMON GREY TREEFROG

GREEN AND GOLD BELL FROG

NORTHERN CRICKET FROG

SPRING PEEPER

LUTZ'S PHYLLOMEDUSA

EUROPEAN GREEN TREEFROG

GOLDEN ARROW-POISON FROG

MARSUPIAL FROG

True Frogs I

NAME: **South African Bullfrog,** *Pyxicephalus adspersus*
RANGE: **E. South Africa**
HABITAT: **open grassland (veld); in temporary puddles when available**
SIZE: **up to 20 cm (7¾ in)**

The largest South African frog, this bullfrog has a stout body and broad head. The male usually has a yellow throat while the female's is cream. On its lower jaw are toothlike projections which it uses to restrain struggling prey such as mice, lizards and other frogs. Its hind toes are webbed, but the front toes are not.

A powerful burrower, it spends much of the year underground but comes to the surface after heavy rain to breed. Males call from a breeding site in shallow water, where females then lay their many eggs, one at a time.

NAME: **Striped Grass Frog,** *Ptychadena porosissima*
RANGE: **Africa: central tropical areas to E. South Africa**
HABITAT: **marshy areas**
SIZE: **4 cm (1½ in)**

This small, streamlined frog has a pointed snout and a ridged back. Its hind limbs are powerful, making it a good jumper and strong swimmer. Secretive in its habits, it often lives among dense vegetation.

Breeding males sit among aquatic vegetation and call to females with a rasping sound, which is amplified by their paired external vocal sacs. Their mates lay their eggs, one at a time, in the water. The eggs float at first and then sink to the bottom; the tadpoles swim and feed near the bottom.

NAME: **Marsh Frog,** *Rana ridibunda*
RANGE: **S. W. Europe: S. W. France, Spain and Portugal; E. Europe: Germany, east to Russia and Balkans**
HABITAT: **ponds, ditches, streams, lakes, rivers**
SIZE: **up to 15 cm (6 in)**

The marsh frog is one of the several noisy, aquatic, gregarious green frogs found in Europe. Apart from its colour, this long-legged frog is easily distinguished from the brown frogs by the external vocal sacs at the sides of its mouth. Most of its life is spent in water, but it will come out on to banks or float on lily pads. As well as catching invertebrate prey, these large frogs feed on small birds and mammals.

Marsh frogs sing night and day and are particularly vocal in the breeding season, when they make a variety of sounds. They mate in April or May, and females lay thousands of eggs in several large clusters.

RANIDAE: True Frog Family

There are 500 to 600 species in this family, found almost world-wide on every continent except Antarctica, but sparsely represented in Australasia and the southern parts of South America. Typically, these frogs have slim, streamlined bodies and pointed heads. Their hind legs are long and hind feet extensively webbed. They are usually smooth-skinned and often brown or green in colour.

Most ranid frogs live near fresh water and enter it readily to find prey or escape danger. A few species, however, can thrive in brackish waters or warm sulphur springs and others have become adapted to a ground-living existence and can burrow like spadefoot toads. Some live in trees and have adhesive pads on their toes for grip when climbing, similar to those of the tree-frogs (Hylidae). All are carnivorous as adults, feeding mainly on insects, spiders and small crustaceans.

Large numbers of ranid frogs congregate at the start of the breeding season and males chorus to attract females to the breeding site. The breeding male develops swollen pads on forelimbs and thumbs with which he grasps his mate's body. As she lays her eggs, he fertilizes them by spraying them with sperm. The eggs are usually surrounded by a jellylike substance which protects them to some degree and prevents dehydration. Although females lay thousands of eggs, many of these are destroyed by adverse conditions or eaten by predators, and relatively few survive to adulthood.

NAME: **Common Frog,** *Rana temporaria*
RANGE: **Europe (including Britain and Scandinavia, but excluding much of Spain and Italy), east to Asia**
HABITAT: **varied, any moist area near ponds, marshes, swamps**
SIZE: **up to 10 cm (4 in)**

European frogs are divided into two groups: green and brown frogs. The brown frogs, of which the common frog is an example, tend to be more terrestrial and have quieter voices than the green frogs. The robust common frog varies in coloration over its wide range, from brown or grey to yellow. It is tolerant of cold and is found up to the snowline in some areas. Much of its life is spent on land, and it rarely enters water except to mate or hibernate.

Breeding occurs from February to April, and males attract females to the breeding sites with their deep, rasping croaks. They mate in water and females lay 3,000 to 4,000 eggs in large clusters.

NAME: **Bullfrog,** *Rana catesbeiana*
RANGE: **E. and central USA; introduced in western areas and in Mexico, Cuba and N. Italy**
HABITAT: **lakes, ponds, slow streams**
SIZE: **9–20.5 cm (3½–8 in)**

The largest North American frog, the bullfrog makes a deep, vibrant call, amplified by the internal vocal sac. Although an aquatic species, it also spends time on land and is often seen at the water's edge. It is most active by night, when it preys on insects, fish, smaller frogs and, occasionally, small birds and snakes. Like all American ranid frogs, it is a good jumper and can leap nine times its own length.

In the north of their range, bullfrogs breed from May to July, but farther south, the season is longer. The female lays 10,000 to 20,000 eggs in water which may float on the surface or attach to vegetation. The eggs hatch in 5 or 6 days, but the tadpoles take 2 to 5 years to transform into adults.

NAME: **Northern Leopard Frog,** *Rana pipiens*
RANGE: **most of northern North America except Pacific coast**
HABITAT: **varied, fresh water to brackish marshes in arid to mountain land**
SIZE: **5–12.5 cm (2–5 in)**

The slim northern leopard frog is a distinctive species, with large spots on its body and prominent back ridges. It is the most widely distributed North American amphibian and the pattern and intensity of its spots vary over its large range. It adapts to almost any habitat near a permanent body of water and is equally accommodating in its diet; insects, spiders and crustaceans are its main food, but this voracious frog will eat almost anything it can find. Primarily a nocturnal species, the leopard frog may sometimes search for food during the day. If disturbed on land, it leaps away in a series of zigzagging jumps to seek refuge in water.

In the north of its range, the breeding season usually extends from March to June, but in southern, arid areas, leopard frogs are ready to breed at almost any time of year whenever there has been sufficient rainfall. Males gather at breeding sites and make low grunting calls to attract females. Each female lays about 20,000 eggs which her mate fertilizes. The eggs then lie at the bottom of the water on submerged vegetation until they hatch about 4 weeks later. The tadpoles metamorphose to adult form in 6 months to 2 years, depending on temperature and conditions.

SOUTH AFRICAN BULLFROG

COMMON FROG

STRIPED GRASS FROG

MARSH FROG

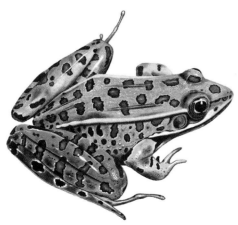

NORTHERN LEOPARD FROG

BULLFROG

True Frogs 2, Sooglossid Frogs, Hyperoliid Frogs

NAME: Wallace's Flying Frog,
Rhacophorus nigropalmatus
RANGE: S. E. Asia
HABITAT: rain forest
SIZE: 10 cm (4 in)

This highly specialized frog is adapted for its habit of gliding from tree to tree in the forest. Its appearance is distinctive, with a broad head, long slim body and elongate limbs. The feet are greatly enlarged and fully webbed, and the tips of the digits expand into large discs. Flaps of skin fringe the forelimbs and heels. All of these modifications add little to the frog's weight but extend its surface area. It can launch itself into the air, webs and skin flaps outstretched like a parachute, and glide gently down to another branch or to the ground. Experiments have shown that, if dropped from a height of 5.4 m (17¾ ft), the frog glides down diagonally for a total distance of 7.3 m (24 ft).

The breeding habits of this extraordinary frog are little known but are believed to be similar to those of others of its genus. Rhacophorid frogs lay their eggs in a mass of foam which makes a kind of nest to protect them from excessive heat while they incubate. The male frog grasps the female and fertilizes her eggs as they are laid in the normal way. But the eggs are accompanied by a thick fluid which the frogs then beat with their hind legs to form a dense, light foam. Surrounded with this substance, the eggs are left on a leaf or branch overhanging water. At hatching time the bubble nest begins to liquify, forming a miniature pool for the emerging tadpoles. In some species, the tadpoles complete their development in this custom-made pool, but in others they drop down into the water beneath.

NAME: Mottled Burrowing Frog,
Hemisus marmoratum
RANGE: N. E. South Africa
HABITAT: open country near pools
SIZE: up to 3 cm (1¼ in)

A stout, squat-bodied frog, this species has a small, pointed head with a hardened snout, used for burrowing. It burrows head-first, pushing into the soil with its snout and clawing its way forward with its strong forelimbs. It is rarely seen above ground, although it can move rapidly on land.

Breeding males establish themselves in small holes, preferably in a mudbank, and call to attract mates. The female excavates an underground nest and lays her large eggs, each surrounded by a thick jellylike substance. When her young hatch some 10 to 12 days later, she tunnels to the nearest water, providing a canal for the tadpoles, which then complete their development in water.

NAME: Bush Squeaker, *Arthroleptis*
wahlbergi
RANGE: S. E. South Africa
HABITAT: coastal and inland bush among leaf litter and low vegetation
SIZE: up to 3 cm (1¼ in)

This small, rounded frog is a land-dwelling species. Its legs are short but its digits, particularly the third on each foot, are elongate, well-suited to searching through vegetation for prey.

The bush squeaker's breeding habits, too, are adapted to its terrestrial existence. The eggs, each enclosed in a stiff jelly capsule, are laid among decaying vegetation. There is no tadpole stage; metamorphosis takes place within the capsule and tiny froglets emerge about 4 weeks after laying.

HYPEROLIIDAE:
Hyperoliid Frog Family
The hyperoliids are a group of climbing frogs, closely related to the ranid frogs. They differ from them in possessing adaptations for climbing similar to those of the hylid frogs: each digit on the hyperoliid frogs' feet has a zone of cartilage which allows greater flexibility in the use of the adhesive disc at the tip when climbing.

Most of the 52 species in this family live in Africa, often among rushes and sedge near fresh water.

NAME: Arum Lily Frog, *Hyperolius*
horstockii
RANGE: South Africa: S. and W. Cape Province
HABITAT: swamps, dams, streams, rivers, with vegetation
SIZE: up to 6 cm (2¼ in)

The long-limbed arum lily frog has distinctive bands running from its snout along each side. A good climber, its feet are equipped with expanded, adhesive discs and are only partially webbed. The concealed under-surfaces of the limbs are orange, and these bright areas are momentarily revealed if the frog is disturbed by a predator. The frog then freezes in an inconspicuous posture with its flash colours hidden, while the predator continues to look for the bright orange frog it was hunting. The rest of the body changes colour according to conditions, becoming a light cream in bright sun and dark brown in shade. This helps the frog control its body heat by either reflecting or absorbing the sun's rays.

Courting males often climb up on to arum lilies to call to females. They then mate in water, where the small clusters of eggs are laid on submerged water plants.

NAME: Gold Spiny Reed Frog, *Afrixales*
brachycnemis
RANGE: South Africa: E., S. E. and S. coastal regions
HABITAT: pools, swamps
SIZE: 2 cm (¾ in)

Also known as the golden leaf-folding frog, this tiny, slim amphibian, equipped with adhesive discs on each digit, is a good climber. Its back may be covered with tiny dark spines, hence one of its common names; this feature is common in frogs in the south of the range but rare in the north.

Breeding males take up position among reeds or on water-lily leaves in pools or *vleis* (temporary, rain-filled hollows) and call to females. The female frog lays a small batch of eggs on a leaf above or below water level. Once the eggs are fertilized, the leaf is folded over and the edges are glued together with sticky secretions from the female's oviduct. When the eggs hatch, the tadpoles emerge from the leaf-nest into the water, where they complete their development.

SOOGLOSSIDAE:
Sooglossid Frog Family
The origins and relationships of the frogs of this small family, all found in the Seychelles, have been a matter of contention, but analysis of their anatomy leads most taxonomists to conclude that they are related to the ranid frogs.

NAME: Seychelles Frog, *Sooglossus*
sechellensis
RANGE: Seychelles: Mahé and Silhouette Islands
HABITAT: moss forest on mountains
SIZE: up to 2.5 cm (1 in) Ⓘ

The tiny Seychelles frog has thin, weak front limbs but more powerful hind limbs, with long digits on its feet. It is mainly ground-dwelling and lives in rotting plant matter on the forest floor, needing water for only a short phase of tadpole development. It feeds on small invertebrates.

The frogs breed in the rainy season. The female lays her eggs in small clumps of gelatinous substance on moist ground. The male guards the eggs and when, after 2 weeks incubation, they hatch, the tadpoles wriggle on to his back. The tadpoles respire through their skin and do not have gills; they are protected from dehydration by mucous secretions on the male frog's back. Most of their development takes place here, but they are carried to water, to spend a brief period there completing their metamorphosis before returning to land as adult frogs.

WALLACE'S FLYING FROG

GOLD SPINY REED FROG

BUSH SQUEAKER

ARUM LILY FROG

MOTTLED BURROWING FROG

SEYCHELLES FROG

Index

Index

Classification of Reptiles and Amphibians

CLASS REPTILIA: **Reptiles**
Order Chelonia: Turtles and Tortoises
Family Emydidae: Emydid Turtles
Family Testudinidae: Tortoises
Family Chelydridae: Snapping Turtles
Family Kinosternidae: Mud Turtles
Family Carettochelyidae: New Guinea Plateless River Turtle
Family Dermatemyidae: Central American River Turtle
Family Platysternidae: Big-headed Turtle
Family Cheloniidae: Marine Turtles
Family Dermochelyidae: Leatherback Turtle
Family Trionychidae: Softshell Turtles
Family Pelomedusidae: Greaved Turtles
Family Chelidae: Matamatas

Order Crocodilia: Crocodiles, Alligators and Gavial
Subfamily Crocodylinae: Crocodiles
Subfamily Alligatorinae: Alligators and Caimans
Subfamily Gavialinae: Gavial

Order Rhynchocephalia: Tuatara
Family Sphenodontia: Tuatara

Order Squamata: Lizards and Snakes
Family Iguanidae: Iguanas
Family Agamidae: Agamid Lizards
Family Chamaeleonidae: Chameleons
Family Gekkonidae: Geckos
Family Pygopodidae: Scaly-foot Lizards
Family Xantusiidae: Night Lizards
Family Teiidae: Teiid Lizards
Family Scincidae: Skinks
Family Lacertidae: Lacertid Lizards
Family Cordylidae: Girdled and Plated Lizards
Family Dibamidae: Old World Burrowing Lizards
Family Anguidae: Slow Worms and Alligator Lizards
Family Anniellidae: California Legless Lizards
Family Xenosauridae: Crocodile Lizards
Family Helodermatidae: Gila Monster
Family Varanidae: Monitors
Family Lanthanotidae: Earless Monitor
Family Amphisbaenidae: Amphisbaenids

Primitive Snakes:
Family Leptotyphlopidae: Thread Snakes
Family Typhlopidae: Blind Snakes
Family Anomalepidae
Family Aniliidae: Pipe Snakes
Family Uropeltidae: Shieldtail Snakes
Family Xenopeltidae: Sunbeam Snake
Family Boidae: Pythons and Boas
Family Acrochordidae: Wart Snakes

Advanced Snakes:
Family Colubridae: Colubrine Snakes
Family Elapidae: Cobras and Sea Snakes
Family Viperidae: Vipers
Family Crotalidae: Pit Vipers

CLASS AMPHIBIA: **Amphibians**

Order Urodela: Newts and Salamanders
Family Cryptobranchidae: Giant Salamanders
Family Hynobiidae: Asiatic Land Salamanders
Family Salamandridae: Newts and Salamanders
Family Ambystomatidae: Mole Salamanders
Family Amphiumidae: Congo Eels
Family Proteidae: Olm and Mudpuppies
Family Sirenidae: Sirens
Family Plethodontidae: Lungless Salamanders

Order Apoda: Caecilians
Family Caeciliidae
Family Typhlonectidae
Family Ichthyophidae
Family Scolecomorphidae

Order Anura: Frogs and Toads
Family Rhinophrynidae: Mexican Burrowing Toad
Family Pipidae: Pipid Frogs
Family Microhylidae: Narrow-mouthed Frogs
Family Discoglossidae: Discoglossid Frogs
Family Ascaphidae: Tailed Frogs
Family Pelobatidae: Spadefoot Toads
Family Myobatrachidae: Myobatrachid Frogs
Family Heleophrynidae: Ghost Frogs
Family Leptodactylidae: Leptodactylid Frogs
Family Rhinodermatidae: Mouth-brooding Frog
Family Bufonidae: Toads
Family Brachycephalidae: Gold Frog
Family Hylidae: Treefrogs
Family Ranidae: True Frogs
Family Sooglossidae
Family Hyperoliidae

Bibliography

The following books and articles were particularly helpful during the preparation of *Reptiles and Amphibians*:

Arnold, E. N., and J. A. Burton. *A Field Guide to the Reptiles and Amphibians of Britain and Europe*. Collins, 1975.

Behler, J. L., and F. W. King. *The Audubon Field Guide to North American Reptiles and Amphibians*. Knopf, 1979.

Bellairs, A. d'A. *The Life of Reptiles*. Vols. 1 and 2. Weidenfeld and Nicolson, 1969.

Boulenger, G. A. *Catalogues of the Amphibians and Reptiles in the Collection of the British Museum*. 9 Vols. 1882–1896.

Carr, *A Handbook of Turtles*. Comstock Publishing Associates, 1952.

Cochran, D. M. *Living Amphibians of the World*. Hamish Hamilton, 1961

Cochran, D. M. *Frogs of Southeastern Brazil*. U.S. National Museum Bulletin 206, 1954.

Cochran, D. M. and C. J. Goin. *Frogs of Colombia*. U.S. National Museum Bulletin 288, 1970.

Cogger, H. G., *Reptiles and Amphibians of Australia*. A. H. and A. W. Reed, 1979.

Conant, R. *A Field Guide to the Reptiles and Amphibians of Eastern and Central North America*. Houghton Mifflin, 1975.

Cott, H. B. Scientific Results of an enquiry into the ecology and economic status of the Nile Crocodile in Uganda and Northern Rhodesia. *Trans. Zool. Soc. Lond.* 29 211–356.

Deoras, P. J. *Snakes of India*. National Book Trust, 1978.

Fitzsimmons, V. F. M. *Snakes of Southern Africa*. Purnell and Sons, 1962.

Fitzsimmons, V. F. M. *The Lizards of Southern Africa*. Transvaal Museum, 1945.

Goin, C. J., O. B. Goin and G. R. Zug. *Introduction to Herpetology*. Freeman, 1978.

Gow, G. F. and S. Swanson. *Snakes and Lizards of Australia*. Angus and Robertson, 1977.

Grzimek, B. *Grzimek's Animal Encyclopedia*. Vols 5 and 6. Van Nostrand Reinhold Company, 1973.

International Union for Conservation of Nature and Natural Resources. Red Data Book: Vol. 3 *Amphibia and Reptilia*.

Loveridge, A. *Reptiles of the Pacific World*. Macmillan Co., 1945.

Martof, B. S. *Amphibians and Reptiles of the Carolinas and Virginia*. University of North Carolina Press, 1980.

Menzies, J. *The Common Frogs of Papua New Guinea*. University of Hawaii Press, 1975.

Mertens, R. *The World of Amphibians and Reptiles*. George Harrap and Co., 1960.

Parker, H. W. *Snakes*. Robert Hale, 1963.

Parker, H. W. and A. G. C. Grandison. *Snakes — a natural history*. British Museum (Natural History) and Cornell University Press, 1977.

Passmore, N. I. and V. C. Carruthers. *South African Frogs*. Witwatersrand University Press, 1979.

Phelps, T. *Poisonous Snakes*. Blandford Press, 1981.

Pope, C. H. *The Reptiles of China*. American Museum of Natural History, 1935.

Porter, K. R. *Herpetology*. W. B. Saunders and Co., 1972.

Pritchard, P. C. H. *Encyclopedia of Turtles*. T. F. H. Publications Inc., 1979.

Rooij, N. de, *Reptiles of the Indo-Australian Archipelago*. E. J. Brill, Vol. 1, 1915, Vol. 2, 1917.

Rose, W. *The Reptiles and Amphibians of Southern Africa*. Maskew Miller, 1962.

Schmidt, K. P. and R. F. Inger. *Living Reptiles of the World*. Hamish Hamilton, 1957.

Sharell, R. *The Tuatara, Lizards and Frogs of New Zealand*. Collins, 1966.

Stebbins, R. *A Field Guide to Western Reptiles and Amphibians*. Houghton Mifflin, 1966.

Storr, G.M. *Lizards of Western Australia*. University of Western Australia Press, 1981.

Street, D. *Reptiles of Northern and Central Europe*. Batsford, 1979.

Taylor, E. H. The Amphibian Fauna of Thailand. *Univ. Kansas Science Bull*. 63, 1962.

Taylor, E. H. *The Caecilians of the World*. University of Kansas Press, 1968.

Acknowledgements

The Publishers received invaluable help during the preparation of *Reptiles and Amphibians* from: Heather Angel, who lent us reference slides; Angus Bellairs, who gave advice; Dr H. G. Cogger, who lent us reference slides; Zilda Tandy, who assisted with reference research; the staff of the Herpetology Department of the Natural History Museum, London, particularly Colin McCarthy and Barry Clarke, who allowed us access to specimens and reference; the staff of the Science Reference Library, London.

Filmset in Goudy by Filmtype Services Limited, Scarborough, North Yorkshire.
Origination by Gilchrist Brothers Limited, Leeds